TRIPTYCH

TRIPTYCH

April Vinding

WIPF & STOCK · Eugene, Oregon

TRIPTYCH

Copyright © 2016 April Vinding. All rights reserved. Except for brief quotations in critical publications or reviews, no part of this book may be reproduced in any manner without prior written permission from the publisher. Write: Permissions, Wipf and Stock Publishers, 199 W. 8th Ave., Suite 3, Eugene, OR 97401.

Wipf & Stock
An Imprint of Wipf and Stock Publishers
199 W. 8th Ave., Suite 3
Eugene, OR 97401

www.wipfandstock.com

PAPERBACK ISBN: 978-1-4982-9253-5
HARDCOVER ISBN: 978-1-4982-9255-9

Manufactured in the U.S.A.

Scripture quotations, unless otherwise indicated, are taken from the Holy Bible, New International Version®, NIV®. Copyright ©1973, 1978, 1984, 2011 by Biblica, Inc.™ Used by permission of Zondervan. All rights reserved worldwide. www.zondervan.com The "NIV" and "New International Version" are trademarks registered in the United States Patent and Trademark Office by Biblica, Inc.™

Epigraph from "St. Thomas Didymus" by Denise Levertov, from *A Door in the Hive*, copyright © 1989 by Denise Levertov. Reprinted by permission of New Directions Publishing.

The quotation regarding the Grand Inquisitor comes from page 243 of *The Brothers Karamazov* by Fyodor Dostoyevsky, translated by Constance Garnett, published by W.W. Norton and Company, New York, 1976.

The French quotation is John 21:25 from La Bible Du Semeur (The Bible of the Sower) Copyright © 1992, 1999 by Biblica, Inc.® Used by permission. All rights reserved worldwide.

For Ella Joy, who restores hope.
May you grow in the hum and be spared the clatter.

>   I witnessed
>   all things quicken to color, to form,
>   my question
>   not answered but given
>   its part
>   in a vast unfolding design lit
>   by a risen sun.
>
> DENISE LEVERTOV, "ST. THOMAS DIDYMUS"

CONTENTS

Prologue: 3 | 1
Fathers | 3
Sons | 31
Holy Ghosts | 83

Acknowledgments | 133
Discussions Questions | 136
Notes | 139

PROLOGUE: 3

Triptych always sounded like something to stumble over, edges to catch the nails on your toes and the jab of a turned ankle on the brink. A cozy, disturbing similarity to 'cryptic.' But the shape itself is not a secret.

'Trinity' says this faith is full of threes. A number with both points and curves—where each always seems to look like the other until, open, you find yourself hanging from a sheet metal angle stuck under your ribs or, armed, you're whirled open by a satin curve, spun on your seat, looking right back where you came from.

'Triad' says this faith is bound. If two heavenly bodies, one pull to the core. If two coals on the earth, one flash in the sky. Burn oak, it will amber; burn ether, there's azure. There's no way to keep the fuel from coloring the flame. So I've looked at the fuel, and chosen. Looked at the flame to choose.

'Triune' says competition is not the problem. Instead, it's the clutter—all that collects inside the angles.

The shape of this faith is a triptych all its own: maybe a reflection of what should be worshiped, maybe an object of art all by itself. But even if this structure is a picture of the divine, it's painted on wood with squeaky hinges. Some days, it seems ridiculous there need to be lines etched on to show where the figures are looking. Other days, those scratches are the only guides I have to God. But what the shape means is I can't really call my faith a journey—this is not a pilgrimage down a narrow road. Because of this divine shape, faith is a container that holds a match: a puzzle, a flame, a fight.

When I wonder about the struggle—to fit a shape, a name, an expectation—I wonder if my struggle will end up being my proof. Because struggle needs a preposition: with. I've been angry with God, crushed, lovesick, offended, but it's always been something. Faith has been a puzzle about, a flame for, a fight to.

I don't know what follows the prepositions. But I do notice the three: the article that makes singular, the noun that makes tangible, the preposition that makes motion. Phrases with both points and curves. I've found myself hanging from sheet metal angles, and now, full of scars, I'm whirled open by a satin curve, looking back where I came from.

As I look back, I see more than I saw the first time through. The edges of this altarpiece are neither right nor varnished, but I can see the interfolding, overlapping leaves. More lines than I'd like point to me than to God. And I don't know yet if what's burnished shows only my hands worrying the holy. What I do know is this: this puzzle, this flame, this fight makes a shape with counterpoint. As much as others might say (and I would say myself) parts are far from worship, this faith has been an instrument of something: a shape with just enough tension to hold me in.

FATHERS

Surrounded for miles by cornfields and woodlands, the farm was a worn spot in a pair of old jeans. Dusty and threadbare in the center—where gravel showed through like the knee-skin of the earth—the house, barn, and garden were stitched around the grass fringes under the crisp and stacked Minnesota sky. The mile-long driveway spooled from the square seam of the county roads to the house: a piece of worn 70s embroidery, the best efforts of a 23-year-old farm wife to craft style from hand-me-downs and a little colored thread. The barn, corrugated steel with button ventilation chimneys, sat outside the homemade curtains and past the yard and its rusting and prized swing set. The garden, a calico quilt square, laid in leafy stitches on the bottom side of the gravel scuff, a never-ending sampler.

Corn and soybeans in the fields, foxtails and wild grapevines in the ditches, the wind making everything wave just a little, the sun and the sky making smells: this place is the first home I remember.

The farm was tired, but the little family in it, mine, marched to the blooming of tomato plants and the drying of the tasseled corn. The fields were our calendar, marking days and seasons as they checkered the land, and the farm itself our timepiece, the round face of hours circling barn, garden, home. And as much as it's been said before, it was true. This place was my first world: the canvas and the blank staff, the open book, the unrecited chant. It was, as Eliot says, the place we start from.

My father, slim and brown, his loose hair wavy and faded like his jeans, roamed the hazy light of the barn in the early mornings. In his spattered Red Wing work boots and Pioneer cap, he moved though the rows of sow stalls under the low ceiling, hot when the afternoons were hot and stoic when it was cold. A red paisley handkerchief hung out his back pocket for wiping his hands and glasses, the square brunette plastic of the 70s, and a pair of work gloves flopped from his right jacket pocket. If you caught him in the late afternoon in the dusty air of the barn, standing in the corridor of hay and rust-colored gates, it was hard to find him, to pick him out. Not because, like some men, his work suited him so well, but because he blended in with the light. Maybe it was simply he was as dusty as the air around him, but looking for him I always had to start down low, let my eyes run across the straw-scattered floor, and find his shoes: brown, scuffed, solid. Then, there he'd be, looking back at me, some kind of far-off question in his eyes.

I always had to search to find my father. In the barn in my elastic-waisted jeans or at church in a cotton floral dress and patent leather shoes, it wasn't hard for me to see him, but it was always the seeing of watching. Watching him stand in a brown suit by the carpeted stairs of the sanctuary and nod in conversation with a few of the men, the deacons, his brows furrowed over marble-blue eyes. Or watching him jog over to help Mrs. Mattson carry a great dish of foil-covered casserole across the leafy parking lot.

My mother, I didn't watch; her presence more like a smell than an image, an aroma to live in, she was the given, burlap warp to my weaving, shuttling weft. We've always looked so much alike—small-framed, large-eyed, with slender Welsh noses and small busy hands—people recognize me instantly as 'one of Diane's girls.' My mother and I look and sound the same, but I am a daughter with her father's substance. Even from the time I was young, barely to his knees, Dad and I have swung out from my mother's quiet cord looking at each other past her fibers, our shared complement.

It may sound demeaning, giving my mother the substance of essence, only the weight of an anchor. But in it she's blessed. Because she's never been a symbol. Her chestnut hair and light coffee alto have always only stood for her: Mom, Diane. My father and I have had the great struggle of being to each other symbols. And so it is, we've watched. I watched because it suited me and because it answered me; they said in church God was like a father, so I had every reason for watching mine.

I watched especially at the beginnings and ends of days, the spaces where he had to cross boundaries, the moments between roles. From the wobbly dining room table, behind plastic cups and slick paintbrush, I would stop swinging my legs and try to see the slice between provider, father—what he was when he wasn't supposed to be anything. This, I thought, the moment between gears, was the place to find the tenor of identity. A difference or a habit, when none was required, would show me the motor behind action, the vision that framed decision. From before I was old enough to think it, I believed this was the place to test where father linked to Father.

At the end of each day on the farm, when afternoon errands and chores were finished, my parents would meet each other in the kitchen, each empty-handed. Mom would raise her heels off the scuffed linoleum, and I would watch my father lean his neck down and their thin lips would touch. They always kissed with their eyes open: hers quiet but wide like they'd met too many flashes in the dark, his squinting like he'd spent his life examining the sun. I've always known my eyes, older, would be split between them: externally, large and round like Mom's, internally, ground and sharpened by hard light.

My parents never lingered or rushed, but ended their kisses with the snap of their lips separating, a click like a latch rejoining. Then she would go back to stirring a bubbling skillet and he would walk into the house to clean up, both of us watching him go, while I puzzled out which pieces of life were which father's choice. Even in my small mind, marking out the territories of love and duty.

The honey-paneled room is bright, Sunday morning sunshine tapping through the glass block of the high basement windows. Rows of folding chairs face the long wall and in the far corner, on the edge of the kitchen serving window, an old aluminum percolator puffs and steams next to a stack of Styrofoam cups and a cut-glass sugar dish. The room is bright and full in the way only children's voices can redeem a tired, yellowed space.

> *Jesus wants me for a sun-BEAM, to shine for him each day,*
> *In ev'ry way try to please HIM, at home, at school, at play.*

> *A sun-beam, a sun-beam, Jesus wants me for a sunbeam,*
> *A sun-beam, a sun-beam, I'll be a sunbeam for him.*

In the front row stands a familiar little girl, her eyes like a swirl of blue and brown paint on a palette or a photograph of blooming nebula deep in the fecundity of space. Her cheeks are like apricots, round and still soft with baby fuzz and her brown hair bobs around her cheeks and brows like a cap. She sings with her mouth wide open, her nose pressing up as her throat opens for the high notes. She's like the smallest bird in a forest singing simply because birds sing.

> *Jesus wants me to be lov-ING, and kind to all I see,*
> *Showing how pleasant and happ-Y, his little ones can be.*

She looks around as she sings, her arms at her sides, her gaze touching the posters of Bible stories on the walls. Jonah and the whale, David and Goliath, Jesus with loaves and fishes. They all look like coloring book pages with the black outlines filled in flat colors. There are no shades on anything and Jesus and Peter, and the three women at the tomb, stand facing each other like simple facts, without backgrounds or context. The little girl knows all these stories by heart.

> *I'll be a sunbeam for Je-SUS, I can if I just try,*
> *Serving him moment by mom-ENT, then live with him on high.*

> *A sun-BEAM, a sun-beam, Jesus wants me for a sunbeam,*
> *A sun-BEAM, a sun-beam, I'll be a sunbeam for him.*

A woman in a flowered skirt asks the children to sit and the little girl climbs on her chair. It makes her hands smell like pennies. Her dress sticks out from her knees as she waves her ankles. She's always been small for her age, surprising women and old farmers in the grocery store when she speaks to them in full sentences. The woman in the flowered skirt sits next to an empty board propped on a chair and covered with olive flannel. She picks up a paper cutout and sticks it to the middle of the board.

"Who can tell me what this is?" she asks the children.

"Lion!" "A lion!"

"Has anyone ever seen a lion?" she asks, looking back and forth to meet the eyes of the older children in the back rows and the younger ones in front. Several shake their heads. "Well, today we're going to learn the story of Daniel, a man who had to spend the night with a bunch of lions. Joshua, sit down in your chair."

"But I can't see."

"Then come sit in the front on the floor here." Joshua, a young boy in a striped shirt, brown pants, and blonde crew cut runs around the outside to sit on the floor.

"Daniel," the woman in the flowered skirt says as she takes down the lion and puts up a picture of a man with a beard and long blue robe and sandals, "lived in a city called Babylon and worked for the king." The little girl looks at the man on the flannel board carefully, her eyebrows crinkled as she listens. "The king's name was Darius—can you all say 'Darius'?" The little girl mouths the word. The woman smooths a cutout of a man with a crown onto the flannel.

"Good," the woman in the flowered skirt continues. "Well, Daniel worked very hard for King Darius and the king put him in charge of the whole kingdom." She reaches to the floor and picks up a cutout of a gold sash with colored stones in it and places it across Daniel's shoulders. The cutout slips and flutters to the floor. She picks it up and holds it between her fingers and looks out at the children: "But, the other men working for the king were jealous of Daniel." The little girl fixes her round eyes on the new cutout of a group of three men.

"The men convinced King Darius to pass a law saying no one could pray to anyone other than the king for a month. But three times every day, Daniel went up to his bedroom and prayed to

God, just as he was supposed to. The other men went and told the king. King Darius was very sad because Daniel was his friend, but the other men insisted he had to be punished because of the law. So that night, Daniel was put in with the lions." She pauses. The woman removes everything from the board but Daniel and puts cutouts of lions all around him. Close enough they could touch. The little girl frowns at the flannel board.

"But, Daniel prayed to God and God sent an angel to close the lion's mouths." The woman puts up a picture of an angel, tall and blonde with big white wings and a sword at its side, beside Daniel. "When the king came back the next morning, he found Daniel safe and sound." She removes the lions and puts the king next to Daniel then smooths the gold, jeweled sash over Daniel's shoulders again. The little girl stares at the cutouts on the board, at Daniel and his sash, as she listens. The woman puts both her hands in her lap and looks again at the children. "Daniel was faithful to God, even when it was hard. He obeyed God's word, did his duty, and God showed his love to Daniel by giving him protection."

A shuffling begins above the children's heads and the brush of conversation scuffles down the stairs. The service is finished and the adults—farmers, feed vendors, the owner of the A&W, and their wives—are chatting and moving toward the basement. The children begin to shift in the metal chairs. The percolator pops and the top rattles. The little girl keeps looking at Daniel, her mouth open like a hungry bird. The children get up to find their parents and the woman in the flowered skirt gathers the cutouts from the floor. As she bends to pick them up, Daniel's sash flutters down again.

The little girl's mother comes to pick her up and the men begin folding the chairs and leaning them against the wall as the women peel plastic wrap from trays of frosted and unfrosted zucchini bread.

"Hi, Sweetie—should we go get Megan and Mindy from the nursery?" Her mother's voice is quiet and young like she'd only begun using it recently.

The little girl turns around and climbs backward off the chair. Her mother picks her up under her shoulders and lifts her to her hip. They walk toward the upstairs nursery to get the little girl's sisters. "What did you learn in Sunday school today, Sweetheart?"

Faithful: love, protection.

We lived in the country, God's country, where Bible Belt and Bread Basket were not demographic or economic but theological. Bread, yeasty and rising, its belly stretching in the bowl, came from hands I knew: seed to soil to a green Tupperware measuring cup and a glass bowl on a familiar cream countertop. The smooth black belt in a deacon's jeans or parched leather on his Bible came from helping cattle birth on New Year's and chasing cows from a frozen pond that Thursday in February. Things beyond the grasp of calloused fingers were in God's hands, and there was no in-between because no one else was involved. Provisions were evidence of hard work and Provision. Like heredity, a difficult but direct simplicity. Sometimes it took a while to parse out where the responsibility lay, but, in the end, there were only two choices.

Every day on the farm, Dad came in to have lunch. He'd wash up to his elbows and we'd all sit up to the table by a streak of sunlight piled on the floor glowing through the yellow gingham curtains. He'd pray, or we'd say "God is great, God is good, and we thank him for our food. A-men" and Megan and Mindy, with their fine hair and liquid eyes, would get to "Amen" a beat behind. We'd eat apples and pickles and sandwiches with Mom's garden tomatoes. Every day, Mom asked Dad what he wanted to drink; every day he said milk. After we ate, Mom laid Meg and Mindy down for naps and Dad would sit in the battered recliner and stretch out his legs. The brown and avocado chair leaked a pouf of dust into the slanting sunlight when he sat, and I'd play Tinker Toys or Lincoln Logs on the carpet while Mom went back in the kitchen to start supper, both of us feeling more secure knowing he was close. Dad would start snoring, narrowly though his Danish nose. The stroganoff would bubble and then we'd hear him: "Shoot." He'd take off his glasses and rub his eyes, crank the leg rest back, and mumble another "shoot," cursing himself for wasting time.

One sunny afternoon while the hotdish bubbled and Dad was gone on errands, Mom took Megan, Mindy, and me out to harvest green beans. Well into motherhood by 23, she used the rhythm of her work—the garden, the house, us girls—as a ladder for climbing out of abuse. She'd left Cedar Rapids for college to escape the alcohol on her father's breath and never moved back. Now, through motherhood and witness of my dad's childhood homestead down the road, she was learning what it could be like to have a family. Each task, learning to can vegetables, sewing us dresses, bringing rhubarb crisp for church fellowship, was a rung toward normalcy, another proof there were things you could stand on.

This afternoon, she tied a kerchief behind her ears and, surrounded by tall sweet corn stalks, wandering cucumber vines, and curling bean bushes, she kneeled on the soil and first pulled weeds. She bent into tendriled bushes, her brown eyes bright under the red kerchief. Megan and Mindy toddled in their pink overall corduroys, and I explored the towering cornstalks, bringing leaves and rocks for them to play with in their grassy camp.

I bopped between standing over their bonneted heads to boss their play and squatting my elfin body next to Mom's nymphish frame. She showed me where to snap the juicy necks of the beans, right under their hats, and I listened to the crack of the fuzzy pods as the juice sprinkled my fingers.

When our bushel basket was almost half-full, Mom flexed her back, fingers draped over her hip, and looked up to shoo a fly. Past her hand she saw a white wall, blanking the landscape, swallowing the trees and phone poles.

She dropped her handful of beans, hefted the basket to her hip and scuttled us to the basement. She sat at the top of the stairs with the phone cord stretched from the kitchen, catching Dad at some register counter or in the FHA office negotiating payments. By the time she had told him what she'd seen, the storm churned like a titan tiller. She hung up when they lost connection, then started us on puzzles while we waited in the gloom.

When it was quiet, we went upstairs and outside. The ground was white. I stepped off the deck and started collecting ice balls in my play teapot and asked if we could keep them. Mindy started crying because she was afraid the kitties weren't safe. Mom took us back inside and we put my filled teapot in the freezer and sat at the kitchen table stringing the beans. The sun came back out, brighter through the oak branches than at lunch. The trees in a seven mile stretch were stripped. The corn crop beyond them stood three inches high.

That night Dad brought roses, three for Mom and one for each of us girls, like there was something to make up for, either on God's behalf or his.

"In those days Caesar Augustus issued a decree that a census should be taken of the entire Roman world." My grandfather's voice begins the familiar story, its tenor timbre the same whether asking for the gravy, telling his sons where to plant, or reading from a columned Bible on his knees. A loose violin string, on the rim of squeaking, his voice is a bending thing. It comes out his lips as if trying to avoid touching his tongue.

"So Joseph went up from the town of Nazareth in Galilee to Judea, to Bethlehem the town of David, because he belonged to the house and line of David."

Grandpa reads the story from an armchair in the farmhouse living room, the long horizontal space between the floor and ceiling lit with the ivory pools of lamps. He is the patriarch in his home: behind him, generations of the faithful, before him, his family. His wife perches on the blonde stone of the hearth, gazing at her usually-busy hands. He reads an important part of the story: genealogy—important because your ancestors say something about the danger and power that live in you. The room rolls out before him with the colored lights on the tree silently blinking off the tinsel. His round belly pushes the Bible to the end of his lap, his head squarish from the missing hair on top and graying stripes on his temples, and his feet awkward and naked in plain stockings on the flat carpet.

"Joseph went there to register with Mary, who was pledged to be married to him and was expecting a child. While they were there, the time came for the baby to be born, and she gave birth to her firstborn, a son . . ."

Dotted across the room, his children are surrounded by their children. The new babies, Adam and Andrea, balanced on crooked forearms, the burst of toddlers, Mandy, Megan, Mindy and Sara, lit on dads' knees, and the two firsts, Jeremy and me, cross-legged on the floor, all of us grandchildren in candy-colored pajamas, the white vinyl soles and toe caps wiggling as we fidget, the zippers snaking from ankle to collarbone, elastic scratching on our wrists.

"And there were shepherds living out in the fields nearby, keeping watch over their flocks by night. An angel of the Lord appeared to them, and the glory of the Lord shown around them, and they were terrified . . ."

We always read about the shepherds—never the gospel with the wise men—because here, surrounded by fields and stars and animals, the shepherds are kin: someone run out to do the chores between supper and presents, someone doing the Christmas milking late after the kids are tucked away on floors and piled in beds together—they are people with no reason to lie, the context of their lives so commonplace that had they imagined the story, there would be no angels or singing, no new stars. To people like this, simply a bountiful crop was miracle enough, proof of abundant love; a leveling of nature was the sign of shirked duty, the result of disobedience or an unworthy sacrifice.

"When the angels left them and had gone into heaven, the shepherds hurried off and found Mary and Joseph, and the baby, who was lying in a manger. When they had seen him, they returned, glorifying and praising God for all the things they had heard and seen, which were just as they had been told."

Grandpa shuts the Bible and puts it on the table beside him. His unaltered voice turns toward his sons and son-in-law, "Boys, time for the chores?"

The men excuse themselves, out to be with their flocks by night, covering in dirty jackets and boots. The women move to do the dishes, divvying leftovers for all the households and putting bones and scraps in an ice cream pail for the farm dogs. We cousins occupy ourselves. Someone starts the coffeepot and I skip around the living room chanting a new song:

> *Just as they'd been told.*
> *Just as they'd been told.*
> *And they found it all—*
> *just as they'd been told.*

In half an hour the men come back, the chores quicker with four sets of hands, knocking snow off their boots and wiping their steamed glasses. Grandpa is still out—finishing some last task. The adults pour coffee and duck into the bathroom to change diapers. Then, Uncle Jeff stops everyone, Grandma in mid-wipe with the flour sack towel dangling from a casserole dish, we cousins weaving through legs and crawling around the floors: "Listen! I think I hear the sleigh bells."

Six little heads swivel and listen. Jeff points, his wavy hair tan like Dad's: "Maybe out the window!" Six small bodies clamber onto the couch and invade the curtains. Dark. Snow. The line of pine trees black against the far gravel road, the space in between empty like the sea at night. Dad calls, winking at Jeff, "I think I hear them too—better check the bedroom." We jump and tumble through the living room, Sara's foot gets smashed, she wails, we stomp and batter back to the bedroom. While we're away someone thumps on the hallway wall. "The roof! That must be the reindeer!" Frothed and vibrating like atoms waiting to be split, our arms and legs are stiff with adrenaline, little fists balled at the ends of our now-too-warm pajamas.

The door smacks. "ho, ho, Hooooo!" Squealing, bumping. "Are there any kids in here or have they all gone to bed?" We scream in response and careen like water bugs, knotting up in ourselves. Father Christmas clomps through the kitchen with his pillowcase bag over his shoulder. He steps into the living room where we are wide-eyed and humming. We've been good and we're desperate for the affirmation.

A few minutes after Santa leaves, Grandpa stomps back in, buzzing his lips and shaking his hair. "Sorry I took so long!"

We burst between the wrapped boxes and run to the kitchen shouting. "Santa came!" "He brought me a present!" "He was fat for the chimney, Papa!" "Santa came!"

"Oh, I'm sorry I missed him. Maybe I'll get to see him next year." Grandpa smiles over his thin teeth. We surge back into the living room and settle in our family clusters, the adults on chairs and couches, we cousins on the floor, the moms on the edges of cushions, ready to help with tape or ribbons.

Grandpa settles back in his armchair, a mug of coffee on the table next to him, and watches his brood: his wife, his sons, his daughters, his daughters-in-law, his son-in-law, his grandsons, his granddaughters. Sits back, the father, the giver of gifts, and watches over.

That spring, Megan and Mindy were in the barn when the pigs got out. A fence latch supernaturally slipped, or wasn't shut tightly enough, and the hundred-pound sows surged from the pens, rioting and shrieking.

Dad shoved through them, his calves crushed between heaving bellies. Mindy yelled, "Daddy! Daddy!" her arms outstretched, while Megan's eyes welled under her bonnet, panic freezing her elbows rigid.

He had brought them to the barn, something unusual—had taken them out to be with him. Whether it was an action of love to be near his daughters or a necessary duty to help Mom now that Grandma had moved out of town, I don't know.

Grandma and Grandpa had moved off their farm, after years of losing money, when Grandpa found a bank for sale in Rockford and decided to gamble on a new life. Though the bank was in a town of only 2,500 and Grandpa was learning the trade hands on, business was going well. He had no trouble relating to the farmer clientele, and everyone needed loans. My parents included. To try to make ends meet, they'd bought a second farm to rent out. But that wasn't enough. Eventually, Dad started selling insurance from a desk in the bank lobby 50 miles away. Several days a week, he would get up in the mornings, haul feed and clean a couple stalls, then walk back to the house to shower and put on his brown suit and tie in time to be in the boardroom by 8:30. The days in between were crowded, hectic, and it may have been easier to overlook details like pen latches.

When Dad reached Meg and Mindy, their fists clenched his jacket and he scooped them up in his arms like lambs. They clung to him as he wrenched his legs through the churning sea of pigs. He'd left them standing on a low ledge when he'd brought them to the barn, a precarious place for three-year-olds—a corner above a concrete floor. The danger of the height had kept them from being crushed.

Dad left the livestock spurting from the pens and brought Megan and Mindy to the house. Mom was excavating the cupboards for her canning supplies, preparing to stretch the garden produce as far into the winter as possible. Meg and Mindy ran for her when Dad set them down. "Call Jeff and have him come fast as he can," he said. "The pigs are out." Megan and Mindy were stunned. I stood in the living room and watched Dad rush back out to the barn.

By the time the hog-flood was dammed, Mom had no use for her Mason jars and six piglets had been trampled. It was clear something important had been protected, but things had also been lost. No one was ungrateful, but in the choice between hard work and Provision, it wasn't clear to me who had failed.

One clouded, fall afternoon I crouched at the backyard stump overturning wet wood dust to find dry underneath. Meg and Mindy were inside with Mom and I had bounded out to the stump in my spring jacket, exhilarated by the blue nylon hood gathered around my face and the cool air on my cheeks. I liked being alone, with no big sister responsibilities, free to touch and absorb the world rather than to give and interpret.

As I wondered at the airy sawdust just below the springy wet surface, Dad walked across the yard from the barn, his face a tanned triangle under his green hat. I was surprised when he stopped in the yard. I saw him often enough: he spent most of his days just feet from the house where we girls did crafts and made cookies, but he worked with the pigs or tractors alone. We only interacted on my ground—in the kitchen, at bedtime in my room, or over dinner—never on his. We shared atmosphere but not space, like two lions naturally distant from each other precisely because we were the same species.

When he came close, he asked if I wanted to swing. I nodded and ran across the yard with my fingers in fists and my arms swishing against the coat, the lining crinkling in my ears. I wrapped dimpled fingers around the cool chains and Dad stood close and gave me a push. He smelled like pigs and dust. On the backswing he grabbed the chains and ran alongside while he pushed, then he thrust his arms up and let me go in the sky.

After a couple flights, he slowed me down and my feet skidded on the dirt under the swing, my toes wiping the soil crumbles back and forth as the seat swayed. He squinted up at the sky and watched a line of geese flash over the yard, arrow across the field, and sail toward the distant trees. I watched him look at the birds. He looked back down from the sky, his eyes still squinted at the corners: "What do you say we walk to the woods? See what's out there?"

The woods were behind the house, a crease in the rippling fields, locked in by acres of worked land. The only way to them was to walk over the fields. I was not allowed near the field that bordered the yard, but at harvest time, yellow cornstalks flew from the combine into the grass and became my brooms and magic wands. I played with them around my stump, knocking the stalks against its sides and tracing the tangled grooves in its weathered flank with tips of leaves. I nodded and we started across the grass, his crusted boots and my pink tennies.

I kicked the leaves as we walked and spattered my shoes with the leftover rainwater locking the leaves together. The field ahead of us was grooved like God had raked it. At the edge of the yard, tufts of seeded grass perforated the line between, marking the boundary. Dad stepped cleanly over them and the seeds caught on my corduroys. When we stepped into the field, my knees pumped and lifted up and down the waves of soil while Dad's boots skimmed the ridges. Uncle Jeff had come to help with what small harvest there was and all the fields around the house were quiet, waiting for the snow.

Another angle of geese called above us. The house and yard looked like a framed picture from this side, a small protected image. I walked up and down, crusty broken stalks bumping my shins and ankles, holding Dad's hand under the open sky. We walked slowly over the stubbled field, a moving wisp breaking the lines on the earth that marked tasks to their places.

When we reached the edge of the fields, Dad lifted me and I put my arms around his neck. My toes bumped against the work gloves in his pockets and the trees ahead held up the clouds like the beautiful, heavy nests of hawks. Soon we stood on the edge of a brook, Dad's boots washed clean of the manure, my hands empty of swing chains or dolls. We could go see the trees, walk through the woods and pick up stones or walnut husks. He could step across the creek and we could see where the geese flew when they left the parks and lawns, what they did when they didn't have to find food and protect a place for their chicks to sleep.

Dad looked out into the woods, his hand reaching out to snap the hollow stem of a cattail before we crossed. He handed me the cattail and I held it heavy in my fist. The outside was soft and dense with velvet. He lifted his heel to cross the gurgling water and said, "We should take some treasures home to show Mom and Megan and Mindy. They'll be sorry they couldn't come with us." He smiled, his lips thin like Grandpa's, his eyes blue like mine.

But when he looked back over the creek to see where we were going, he paused. He squinted at a small red square floating against the cluttered branches at the edge of the trees. I tried to find what he was reading, but only saw a spot of red. I couldn't read the words, but the sign was clear. We shouldn't cross the brook; it was time to go back home.

Dad talked to the trees as we both looked past the brook. "Maybe I should get back to the new piglets—and we wouldn't want to scare the geese away from their nests."

When we stepped back into the yard, Dad set me down and I went back to the swing set to push down the slide. Back in my yard I felt safe and adventuresome, protected by the house and the aspen fluttering over the slide, with the cattail as a new prize to add to my kingdom. I laid it down on the end of the dimpled slide and Dad pushed me again on the swing.

Soon, he had to go back to the barn. He thanked me for going on a walk with him and gave me a kiss on my cool cheek. Then he slipped his work gloves back over his hands. He walked back to the barn, his head up, angled toward the edges of the grass and field and brook. His brows were folded, but I couldn't see what his eyes were focused on. As he crossed back to the gravel of the barnyard, a line of geese called overhead. I looked up at them and suddenly felt confused, not sure if I was happy to be in the square of my yard or not, not sure if I was happy to have left it. Dad watched the geese fly into the woods before walking through the door of the barn; I went over to crouch by my stump, hungry for rippling places with centers, heavy with so many lines.

By fall Dad was driving to the bank nearly every day. The crops weren't making enough money and, even though he had found a buyer for the second farm and was selling a few hogs each month, FHA started sending demand notes. The land he'd planted was pulling away.

When he'd left the farm for the first time, pulling himself away, Dad had gone into the city to college, looking deep into the words he'd grown up with, leaving home to discern if God was calling him into a pastor's ministry. He tried to find God's voice in schooling, but after hints and leadings, there had been no voice from heaven, no fatherly affirmation of a gift held up in open hands. So he went back to the land.

On autumn afternoons in the combine, rolling over the soil shabby and spent, he could have wondered why. Wondered if harvests of grain were his highest entrustment, the task for which God thought him worthy. But on spring days—the land snapped out black and ready, the trees whole again in glossy sun—Dad sat alone in the high cab of the planter and, feeling the space warm in the rays from the sky and waves from the land, could have believed God had guided him to the place he could be most fulfilled. Could have believed he'd been brought back to the land of his fathers to raise his girls and love his wife, to work out a hard but simple living in the landscape of heritage. Could believe that, like the shepherding of Moses and David, the wandering of Elijah, God could use the land to shape and fill a man.

But prophecies came by envelope and soon it was clear even this might be taken. Dad heard FHA was anxious enough they were accepting proposals. So, he walked into the county office and prayed they would accept his: whatever I can sell my farm for is yours. They took it.

When he came home, I couldn't see his face—the line of his lips or his squinting eyes, which would be ridiculous, now, with no distance around them, fixed in the wrong frame of vision. We would move to town; Dad would wear a suit. I wished for the bone of my stump and the flank of the yard, thought about the woods and the sound of the geese. Dad cleaned the fodder off his boots and set them in the square closet between his dress shoes and my pink Kangaroos, something else put away.

The night before we moved, Meg, Mindy, and I jumped on Mom and Dad's mattress in the living room, Meg's self-trimmed hair flopping jagged and lopsided, and Dad put the last box by the door. We'd already eaten supper and packed away the dishes, and our Strawberry Shortcake and Rainbow Brite sleeping bags were laid out in the bedroom. The only other things in the house were five toothbrushes, the couch, Mom's contact case and the record player. Dad came in, surveyed the empty kitchen, and walked into the living room. As he squatted next to the record player his knees cracked like they did when he walked down the stairs. He slid a slip of vinyl from its cardboard sheaf and parchment wrapper and placed it on the turntable. The record started spinning and he picked up the needle, blew the dust off, and cradled it between the grooves.

The needle crackled, laying down the snaps, and Billy Joel began crooning "The Longest Time." Turned away from us, I could see Dad's shoulders sink into the yearning, then his decision to climb up the harmony to be where we were. "Want to dance, girls?"

Meg and Mindy, full of an innocence he was being asked to farewell yet again, ran up and threw their arms around him. He waddled around the living room with a pair of little feet on each shoe. Mom came from vacuuming upstairs to watch, her eyes a thread of assurance that happiness can go on.

When Dad started slowing, Mom asked Meg and Mindy to dance with her. They ran over and she spun them in ballet twirls. Dad scooped me off the mattress. My toes bumped the wallet in his pocket. We started dancing with my legs swinging.

We could both do the yearning, though I couldn't yet say what it was for: a voice in the hall, unwritten music, the fact of miracles and mutual need even without demonstration of their fulfillment. There was nothing I could do for him, and I knew it. But he knew it too.

Dad and I danced until the end of the song and Meg and Mindy twirled themselves dizzy. At the end, Dad set my feet back on the carpet and went to stop the spinning record. Mindy, in a smiling heap on the floor, drunk on vertigo, her cheeks and nose crimson and her eyes wide and glassy shouted, "Again!" Megan and I joined her, jumping from the floor to the mattress and back, the word bouncing and dipping with us, springs in our stomachs and throats. "a-Gain, A-gain, a-Gain, A-gain, a-gAin!" Dad bent, his knees cracking, and moved the needle back. Mom walked toward the couch and saved them both: "Why don't you girls dance? Dad and I will watch."

The music started and all three of us began whirling, necks stretched back, palms up, the dingy speckled ceiling flopping, mixing, swirling as we spun faster, faster. Everything shifting from liquid back to solid as we thumped to the floor, our brains smudging the room back to place.

We sped up on the bridges, the bouncing valves of the background vocals filling our ears with the sound of our eyes. Mom and Dad flopped on the couch and Dad picked up his feathered Bible to make room. This morning he'd been up before everyone and had left it on the couch where he'd done his usual reading. Billy Joel wondered about the boundaries of hope and the virtue of being too far gone to turn back.

Mom and I watched Megan and Mindy smash into each other and spring exactly backwards, two little bodies, one blonde, one brunette, flinging off each other like reflections, their bottoms planted, their feet sprawled straight out facing each other. Mom watched for the quiver of tears. They giggled and turned opposite directions to crawl back up. I looked to see Dad smile at them and caught him with one hand still on his Bible, placing it aside. The burgundy paper cover had gold letters: *Serendipity Study Bible. For groups and lay leaders*. I caught him lingering over it.

The voice in the air put aside consequences, declared willingness to be a fool, and told everyone listening that what happened next came of his want and his intention. Dad turned to give Mom a kiss, his eyes intent as the record spun.

On the left side of the sanctuary, on the outside edge of the light, I can see myself as a little girl sitting beside her mother. The little girl's fingers touch the cover of a hymnal, feeling the painted red bookcloth to the edge of the embossed gold letters. The copperplate capitals have sharp cliff edges and flat smoothed valleys. Her finger settles in the valley and strokes the cool center of the T. It's like the cross on the front wall of the room, above the sunken basin used for baptisms the children walk in dry after Sunday morning service as they jump around the stage steps and hide under the choir chairs.

The sanctuary smells like old hymnals, their edges faded to pink and daubed with inexplicable water spots, the pages cream and knit with the aroma of attics and tape. The congregation tonight is wide and shallow in the varnished pews. The ceiling is low and unspectacular, the carpet and pew cushions scratchy with yellow and green flecks. The back of the church is dark, only the front row of lights is on. In true Protestant fashion, everything here is electrical, practical: there's no candlelight or arched stone—the dark windows are clear paned glass that opens, in the light, to let the summer breezes in for coolness more than atmosphere.

A man with white hair and glasses is talking at the front of the church, in front of a music stand, with the raised pulpit darkened behind him. The little girl knows he's a missionary. She's here alone with her mother, who wanted to hear the man. She's the only child in the room, her mother like a sort of sister, the next youngest in the group of white hair, pleated skirts, and pinstriped overalls. The man speaking uses no microphone. He's come from China and will go back there to keep working on translation.

I see the little girl listen, nested in the seat, her sitting body the same size as the angle of the pew. Two Ls resting exactly in each other. The wood of the pew hurts her back, but she doesn't fidget, she's listening. And thinking.

The man speaks about love and protection. He uses the words 'heaven' and 'Father' and 'darkness' and 'hell.' But 'hell' with a sadness of loss—his voice lowers as he says it—the way people speak of a child or a friend who has not just left but cut ties and run away, not from any building or person called home, but from the place inside themselves that recognizes it.

Small as she is, the little girl can recognize this kind of hurt. It shocks me to see her see it. She thinks it sounds like birds at night. Loons and geese and the loneliness of flight in a dark sky. I know now she'll feel it every time she finds herself in an airplane at night, moon or none, and will wonder at how very close it is to peace, how there could be such a small distance between the deepest kind of good and the unbottomed hollow.

Though she doesn't think this in the church pew, she senses the feather of dark around the back of the sanctuary and the black pressed hard on the window glass. She knows there are two kinds of boundaries—not just between right and wrong—but in all reasons why. She wants them all to be window panes, solid and clear, with the simplicity of being either outside or in. She wants love to be recognizable by noise, to buzz or hum, or duty to give off a smell, like clean porcelain sinks or animals. She wants to know who loves her.

In the church, the white-haired man asks if anyone would like to come to the front. This is an action, a clear separation as easy to read as a window being open or closed. The little girl is scared of hell, but mostly she craves the clarity, somehow wants her body to mark an absolute. She turns to her mother and says, quietly, "I want to go up there."

The mother's heart turns over in her chest. She takes the little girl by the hand and they walk up the side aisle, up the stage steps and into a shadowed corner. There's a shuffling at the front of the church as someone goes to find something: they weren't expecting children. The white-haired man talks to the little girl. He has glasses and a square sort of face with baggy cheeks like a grandfather who always has a book. Someone brings a small pamphlet, the best they could do: a tract with cartoon people drawn in it. The little girl looks at the people in the pamphlet in their balloony red and blue clothes and at the black-lettered words around them. She smells the flat walked-on carpet.

She listens, and she thinks.

She's heard people talk about what it feels like to do this: light, like the moment at the top arc of a pushed swing. She wonders if doing it will help her see why there are storms. Or why Dad brings flowers or stops for signs—because he wants to or because he should. It's important to her to know which.

The little girl breathes through her nose and feels the man's warm hand on her small shoulder. After he finishes talking, she wraps her fingers around each other, closes her eyes and tilts her head. She doesn't feel anything, no swinging, or hear anything, not a hum, so she figures all this must have to do with what you see. With her small nose almost touching her soft knuckles, she prays, decides to become one of the faithful, and frames the world so duty is the entryway to love.

Now that we've moved, Mom and Dad whisper a lot. Dad comes home from the bank in suits and ties, his hair is short now above the shirt collars, and they whisper in the kitchen before dinner. And we don't pray "God is great, God is good . . ." Dad prays quietly thanking God for things like "sovereignty" and "strength." After dinner, Dad sits in the living room with papers from the bank and Mom does dishes in the dark kitchen and tells us to go play in one of the bedrooms. I ask why. Mom says, "Daddy needs some quiet." Mindy says, "Why?" Mom says, "Sometimes it's hard for Daddy to be at work." Megan says, "Why?" Mom says, "It's hard for Daddy to work with Grandpa at the bank right now." Grandpa didn't come to Christmas this winter.

I heard there was an emergency at the bank and Grandma had to call Grandpa when he was away. She started calling all the hotels to find him at his conference. But when the hotel people found his number, a lady answered the phone.

Grandma and Grandpa went to court over the bank. The court said Grandma gets it, and Dad's still going to work there. I wondered at my birthday if that was why Grandpa didn't send a present. I asked Mom if that meant Grandpa didn't love me anymore.

Before she answered, Dad yelled from the corner of the table: "Moo-oo-ooo-Wah-Ah-Ah-Ah!" and Meg and Mindy ran away screaming, "April, run!" "The Monster will get you!" Dad belted the monster laugh again and I ran from my chair to Meg and Mindy. We tore around the house hiding in closets by the sleeping bags or squishing behind the doors. Mindy and I peered through the hinges while Dad stomped up to the door. "Where are those little girls?" he said in Monster voice. We peeked too hard and he caught us through the crack. "I see you! Moo-oo-ooo—Ah-Ah-Ah-Ah!" We were trapped and he caught us and put us in the jail in the entryway. Before he walked away we yelled to Megan: "Megan! Come save us! We're in jail!" We warned her he was coming upstairs to get her. She slid down the stairs on her butt, we heard the thump-thump-thump, then her sharp eyes ran toward us and she tagged our hands.

After our game that night we had birthday cake. It was shaped like an owl with coconut and licorice eyes. Dad said a prayer before

Fathers

I had my wish. He said, "Heavenly Father, thank you for April and how special she is to us. Help her to know that nothing will ever change how much we love her."

I can see the moon out my window tonight. It makes the tops of the cars glow as they drive by. Mom and Dad are saying prayers with Megan and Mindy in their bunk beds. We danced in the living room tonight when Dad got home so Meg and Mindy got to stay up past their bedtime. I came up to put my pajamas on and to crawl under the covers. After Mom and Dad tuck me in, sometimes I get up and turn on the light again so I can write. I keep a notebook with light purple paper and a pencil behind the little sliding door at the top of my bed.

Sometimes it's hard to fall asleep at night. Dad has the same problem. When he sneaks me popcorn after bedtime, he's never surprised I'm still awake. I tell Mom that my body is tired but my mind just keeps going. She asks what I think about but Dad never does. I think he knows that the thoughts are usually big to fit into words and sometimes they feel like things it would be bad to ask.

Even when my mind is quieter, I never know how to lay. I like to lay on my side or my stomach, but neither of those work. On one side, I have my back to the door, and that makes me afraid because I can't see if there was a scary noise and I needed to know if someone was there. On the other side, I have my back to my stuffed animals and I can tell from their eyes that they are a little sad already and putting my back to them would make them more sad. My stomach is most comfortable, but I can't do that because then my back's to God and you should never turn your back on God. So the only thing to do is lay on my back because the devil's down there. It's hard for me to fall asleep on my back, but at least I know it's okay to put my back to the devil. He can get as mad and he wants and that won't change anything. I think.

Lately, I've had a lot of questions for God so before I go to sleep I write them on the purple paper and make sure they have a question mark at the end. I just write one question each night and then I put the pencil and the paper on top of my headboard. I don't understand why God answers some prayers and not others. Like, how I got my Kangaroo shoe out of the storm drain when my leg slipped in, but how we had to move from the farm or how Grandpa doesn't talk to Dad.

Right now I write little, curious questions. Like "What is heaven like?" and "Are there cats there?" Then in the morning I check to see if God wrote an answer there. He hasn't yet, so I don't write any big questions. Questions like, "Do you love me?" I wonder that. Because God loves everybody just because he's God, but I wonder if he loves me all alone. Because even though Dad and Grandpa love each other, Mom says so, Grandpa doesn't love Dad all alone, he just loves him the way he has to.

I just don't think I could write the love me question. Because I don't know what would happen if I already prayed to love God and then he didn't answer.

Last night Mindy came to my room in the middle of the night. She had a bad dream so she ran up the stairs. Most the time we go in Mom and Dad's room when we have bad dreams, but it's scary to wake up mom because she jumps so high. I always sneak across the hall and as soon as I cross the line on the carpet I whisper "*mahhom?*"

Their room is darker than mine and the shadows change as soon as I cross the line on the carpet. When they are sleeping, their room is scarier than mine is. My room has light spots and dark spots, but Mom and Dad's room has lots of grey, nothing is just bright or dark. When Mom doesn't move, I step closer and then check behind me. "*Mahhom?*" Nothing. Then when I'm right next to her I touch her arm, "*mahhom?*" "—HHU?—WHAT?" She's sitting up and loud and her eyes aren't even open. She can't see without her glasses so she reaches for my face to feel if it's me or Megan or Mindy before she opens her eyes. "*It's okay mom I just had a bad dream I just had a bad dream it's okay it's okay*" "Alright Sweetie, *shh*. Grab the blanket on the end of the bed and you can sleep here on the floor, but be quiet so we don't wake up Dad." Someday I'll tell her that she's the one who's so loud.

So, when Mindy came to my room I heard her run up the stairs so I was awake when she came in. I gave her the pink afghan and told her she could sleep on the floor. I should have two blankets because my carpet is crunchy to lay on and it makes pokey marks on your arms and cheek. I was scared too when I heard her coming up the stairs—I looked past her when she was in the doorway to be sure no one was following her. When she was laying down I tried to make sure she didn't see me checking the door. But her scaredness made me less scared. I told her it was okay. "It's okay, Mindy." She believed me.

When I woke up this morning one of the corners in my room had grey in it. It made me wonder if Mom and Dad and God lie sometimes too, to make things more simple, to make us feel better. I wonder if that's okay. And I wonder if lying is something different if you do it because you love someone or because you feel like you have to.

SONS

The sun wrapped around her slim wrist as it rocked over the heads of red geraniums, forward and back, her thin tanned fingers grasping the spent blooms and popping them from the plant. The green, cracking smell of the stems baked off the broken heads and seeped onto Betsy's warm skin. Standing next to my best friend, I bent my shoulders over a white geranium and began plucking too. Two high schoolers, we circled the temporary fence around the seasonal greenhouse unburdening plants of their dead parts. Betsy slipped the crisped buds into her palm until it was full then bent closer to the radiating asphalt and shook them into the base of the pot over moist black soil.

Picking up an obvious metaphor from our surroundings, we talked about what we always talked about: love.

"It just seems like I want too much," I said, unusually tuned to statements rather than questions. Betsy ran her thumb and forefinger over the crown of her head to brush her honey-wheat hair from her narrow face. Her crescent brows open, she nodded to encourage me to keep talking. She was a good listener, attentive.

We always took ourselves seriously, our gaze toward Music, Art, Love even in radio tunes, novels and movies. Raised in different limbs of the Christian church, Lutheran, Evangelical, we'd been dealt serious things from an early age and it upped the ante all around. And both firstborns, every time someone said something was important we believed them. By 18, we'd each already gathered a long list of to-do's and a high wall of expectations: hers about the value of the present, process, beauty, relationship; mine about the planning of the future, standard, outcome, truth.

"I just don't know what's a challenge and what's a sign," I continued. "I've said I love him, and I do. I'm just beginning to wonder about the difference between loving someone and being in love with them. What's the proof someone really loves you? What's the proof you really love them?"

I had been dating Brian since my sophomore year, growing up with him in the relationship. We'd been different in the same surroundings, but now that I was going off to college and he was floating around a tech school, the differences were starting to crescendo. In high school it was fine I sang chamber music while he played guitar with a garage band—we surprised teachers as a pair, but it made us both well-rounded. Now, away from lockers and lunch periods, different pastimes meant different lifestyles. But I loved him. I said I loved him, and that carried some kind of bond.

The nature of love was one of Betsy's specialties, the thread that bound her favorite novels—*The Scarlet Letter, Tess of the D'Urbervilles, My Antonia*—and the topic on which she always had an opinion. We moved to another cluster of pots and I sat on a stray concrete block in front of a wide collection of purple. The spent flowers in it were curled and wet, liable to rot rather than dry. Different risks for different species. I asked for instructions.

Betsy wiped her fingertips on her cut-off shorts and looked at my pot. Her slight frame always made the pockets on the back of her pants seem too big. I wondered if mine looked that way too. She nodded for me to do the same with these pots as the last, her wrist still rocking back over the buds, her fingers moving the leaves as if sorting it, searching for hidden huddles of petals.

"What are these called?" I started pulling the wet twists and dropping them through the plant.

"Petunias—double wave."

We worked for a moment in a strange pause. Even in small things we weren't quite accustomed to her owning the information and experience. She'd always known flowers, but our relationship functioned on the cogs of another machinery. Between us, I was always the one giving advice, introducing the system, functioning like a world-wise older sister. I'm not sure either of us ever wanted that, but when we met she'd walked into a group of people I already knew and the role of presenter had stuck with me and become familiar to us both. She broke the silence, speaking thoughtfully.

"I'm not sure there is a difference, between loving someone and being in love with them."

Her current relationship gave her no reason to distinguish. Jason was a poet and photographer, quirky in his collections and preferences—X-men, Journey—but philosophical, with a curly blonde ponytail. Their relationship was Romantic, full of the flash and drama of the definitive and sublime. I considered ending the conversation to keep from appearing deficient or incapable. My relationship with Brian was beginning to feel like payment on a check. For two years I'd been telling him I loved him, had put his name in the 'Pay to' slot and had knowingly filled in an infinite amount with the four digits. Then I'd signed it, with time, with repetition, with giving and receiving touches that challenged the line of chastity. I'd known all along love meant permanence, loyalty, bending to fit—but expected to feel the job of it at 40 not 18. I decided to try and explain myself more accurately.

"I just feel like there's this whole garden," I said, a little proud for fitting my thoughts into our surroundings. "And it's full of all different things. Some of the things are in the shade and some are in the sun—some of them are going to die, but the problem is I have to choose. But I don't know what I'll miss when it's gone and what I'll wish there was less of. I don't even really know what's all there to begin with. I mean, are the forget-me-nots supposed to die or the roses?"

Betsy nodded. I remembered a page in the front of her planner with her liquid handwriting curled around one of her many garden quotes: Bloom where you are planted. But I had no confidence I'd actually been planted. I felt responsible, like everything was up to me, and the burden of definition was oppressive. Especially with the overlay of faith. The Father was systematic and provisional, but Christ was incarnate, relational—the bridegroom, the ultimate lover. Christian faith was supposed to be a courtship of the soul. Wondering about the boundaries and proofs of love was more than strategizing about the chess game of dating: it was the task of defining belief.

In Betsy's silence, I was suddenly embarrassed by the earnestness in my shallow garden metaphor. She'd probably just been listening, taking to heart, but in case she wasn't, I punned to save my dignity, "Maybe the impatiens are supposed to go."

She didn't laugh. Maybe I'd just turned my struggle trite and destroyed any personal meaning she was making of it. That was the trouble with making metaphor of someone else's world—you might cheapen it.

We moved to the last batch of flowerpots, this bay warmer without streaks of water dribbled over the asphalt from the hose. The sun tumbled everywhere, glinting off the lake across the street and draping my head. Betsy glanced at me to ask her question.

"But why does anything have to die?"

This was where our differences—she with her planner full of last year's calendar pages, me with mine full of next year's—blocked the way. For me, that was the one given. Something always had to die. That was the stone at the center of the fruit of reason: some things were mutually exclusive; some things had to die for others to live. It was irrational to think otherwise.

I nodded thoughtfully and changed the subject. It was about time to get the focus off me anyway.

"How are you doing with the college thing—have you and Jason talked any more about that?"

Betsy stood up straight, her brows compressed in the light. "He really wants to go unattached, to be able to experience everything fully," she said. "And I understand that. If it's meant to be everything will work out."

I brushed my fingers together to smear goo off them, squinting in the metal glare off a passing car. I didn't quite believe Betsy was as nonchalant as she seemed, but we'd established a certain amount of allowable fantasy in our relationship. I let her live in hers and she let me live in mine.

We stood by the corner of the greenhouse for the rest of my visit and talked through her thoughts on the college move.

Surrounded by growing things, she stood believing in anything that proved love, and I stood looking for the proofs that made love believable. The sun shone steady overhead.

The guitar slide bowled into the hot bedroom, rolled its neck, and opened hazy pupils toward the white pebbled ceiling. Harrison laid the carpet for Lennon's ghost, wandering, home. "Free as a Bird" played as the August sun shot in on the window, the single-bulb fixture feeble over the punch of midday light on the far side of the room. I lay on the maroon bedspread smoothing the thin, seamed lines and looking at my fingers while we listened to the Beatles. Brian stood by the stereo, fingering a stick of incense and the dark oily edge of its wood catch as the smoke of the song became its own next best thing.

I could always picture him playing these kinds of songs, the solos of unreleased tracks, fingers curled over frets in the self-reflexive stance of a musician off the stage—denim baggy around his ankles while his feet shuffled over cords and pedals, fraying the hems.

Brian lit the incense, blew out the flame, and came to lie on the bed. I rolled onto my back and lifted one of his palms to massage with my thumbs. The calluses of his fingertips always disturbed me with their fleshy edges and hard domed tips. How could he have the discipline to make them, the imagination for melody, but have neither remain? How could he think and feel deeply enough for music and still be careless?

We watched the ceiling, an old game, looking by default for shapes in the spackling while listening to Smashing Pumpkins, Weezer, or whatever new CD he'd come across.

"See that big dot there? There's a train."

"Like an engine?"

"Uh-huh."

We spent most our afternoons together laying around, either hoping or fearing that sooner or later we'd end up making out.

Mostly he hoped. Mostly I feared. But neither of us said anything before it happened, like making it an accident would excuse us from wondering if we should feel guilty.

"This is a weird one, but that's sort of like a hammer."

"A hammer?"

"See the claw part?"

"Or like a guitar—that could be the bottom curve."

I was afraid I wasn't just bored, but bored with him. I looked from the ceiling to the waving ridges on his calluses and brushed my thumb across the waxy flesh, then turned my neck to look at him. He watched the ceiling, may have thought I was adoring while watching his river-blue eyes search for shapes to surprise me.

I was afraid I was bored with him and he'd be the only good thing I got. I thought about my body: thin, but small-breasted, with boy-jean hips and short enough to be only ever cute. That smart girl with the cute little body. Five inches and two cups short of anybody's dream.

"I love your hands—they're so tiny. Your little knuckles and fingernails."

Brian turned my hand around, petting my fingers over and tucking them into a fist.

He was willing to do all kinds of great things: to dream songs and coffee shop ministries and road trips for when we were fifty, but none of it made it to now. If it happened, it happened. And I needed to relax and let God take care of things.

"Brian?" Carol's voice came through the door. She cracked it open and Brian played with my fingers while his mom asked if I was staying for dinner. I sat up and made lots of eye contact. At my house, we bolted to opposite sides of the couch when one of my parents came downstairs—whether we were fooling around or not. There, all of us were uncomfortable acknowledging bodies had anything to do with relationships.

Carol bent in to put a basket of laundry on the floor: "Brian—this is pot smoking music." We laughed. Brian probably would have been a smoker if anyone had ever bothered to offer him pot, but the idea of me having anything to do with it was ridiculous to us all.

Brian teased, "How would you know, Mom?"

"Well . . ." She trailed off as usual, embarrassed whenever the attention of more than one person focused on her. "Dinner when your Dad gets here," she said and latched the hollow door behind her.

The CD changer jerked and whirred and a Beatle pleaded with his darling. Brian smiled. He wanted me to believe, even if he didn't tell me, he'd never do me harm.

"This is what you were doing with the stereo." Programming the mechanics of a make-out session. All those little actions that weren't quite guilty, weren't totally innocent. We usually played the game in pawns, nudging innocuous pieces around the board, trying to avoid the attention of the judge.

"I have to do something while you think." Brian turned on his side and faced me, fanning my hair around on the bed. "You have to stop worrying so much about everything."

It was hard to know how to respond to him. I did want to stop worrying, to stop wondering what would happen if we messed up and just slept together—to stop wondering if I was living outside the holiness or purity that would open the messages of God. Two years was a long time to date without having sex, but somehow that didn't seem to count. All the things I was doing right still weren't opening the lines. I'd started trying to listen when I was four, but still hadn't heard a single word from the God who wanted to have a personal relationship with me. I wanted to stop worrying if it was my fault.

But I wanted Brian to stop it. I wanted to stop having anything to wonder about, but wanted him to take care of it—to fill up his role as protector, spiritual leader—and stop doing things I'd need to worry about. I wanted him to stop saying he loved me while doing things that proved to me he didn't.

I kept looking at the ceiling. "I'm not worrying, just thinking."

He sat up and caught my eyes. "Here, turn over, let me give you a massage—I learned this new brushing technique."

I turned over and twisted my hair out of the way. Brian sat up on his knees and pushed my shirt up to put oil on my skin.

I sighed and closed my eyes to lie and listen, wondering which of us needed to believe and which might not make it alone.

Three weeks later I moved into a dorm at a Baptist liberal arts college an hour from home. Brian was already down in Hutchinson working at the coffee shop and waiting to start classes again at the tech school. He'd never really made a decision about college, but Hutchinson Tech let students in late and he thought he might be interested video production. For me, the decision of where to go had been easy enough; I was a homebody and believed faith and learning had something to say to each other. Bethel and its commitment to "the integration of faith and learning to translate Christian values to global service" sounded just right.

I carried 18 credits my first semester and went to chapel to hear about making my faith my own. My Bible class illustrated how God's redemptive plan spiraled down from the scope of the world—through the culture and history of the Jewish people and finally into the single, potent person of Jesus Christ—to spiral out again, through individuals, to all humanity and the healing of all creation. The life around me illustrated how messy that turning could be.

I watched girls have Bible study about beauty of the spirit and panic over what to wear for a date. I heard success was less important than faith and that godly, faithful students were dismissed for deficient GPAs. I smelled ink on FIGHT HUNGER posters and rotting from cafeteria bins of wasted food. Frustrated and imbued with *ad fontes* and all those *solas*, I decided I was surrounded by static.

So, in reformation spirit, I hunkered down to unmediated encounter. The world could not be counted on to translate divinity. Incarnation muddled the lines, though, and experience would have to show what loves could be embodied and which were only so many ideals.

Sons

This carpet smells hot. I hope no one else comes in here today, I hate having to share a space for prayer. And I don't want to fall asleep again. But maybe the sleep is more ministering than the prayer, maybe you do it to get my mind out of the way. I hate wondering if I have those dimpled carpet marks on my forehead though when I walk out. It must have been terrible for Moses to come down that mountain and wonder why people were staring at him—to wonder if it was beauty or disfigurement making them gape or whisper, to fear what glory could have done to him. To fear it since fear feels like wishing it wasn't there.

This desperation is stupid. With all the notes on the iron altar here in the dim, the scraps of paper with words and names: mom, cancer; uncle, depression; roommate, cheating fiancée. I shouldn't read them. But they're like relics. Next to the sculpted crown and bread and nails, I want to touch them because the people who put them there have faith enough to put them there. I'd be embarrassed just to do it, even alone. And what if it worked and I got superstitious and then every prayer would have to be scrawled on blue-lined paper and tucked into a certain crevice under the crown of thorns. I'd be a Flannery O'Connor character, one whose faith is ridiculous in its distance from anything deep, someone almost asking for a violent epiphany.

But still, God—, Lord—,

But still, it is my life, what's—that cheesy children's song in the syrupy little girl voice: I cast all my cares upon you. And then, "ask and it will be given to you" with no prerequisites, "for everyone who asks receives." Everyone. And I'm willing to give the credit.

Is this a message? But I could learn the lesson without the loss— could just have it be missing for a little while, could just think it was missing, then come to the point of lesson and find it again. Lesson learned, everything fine.

A computer disk. A ridiculous British Literature term paper. But, three days before the due date? A corrupted file halfway though. A computer crash on the final revision. Then, all redone and the disk lost in the lab? Yellow, without my name on it. Four months to redo in three days. And when is restarting giving up? Is the risk what I'm supposed to take? Don't start writing again out of faith it will show up? Then what, tell Dr. Ritchie I don't have a final paper because I was waiting for a miracle?

And there's cancer not cured, and car accidents on honeymoons, and I want a computer disk to materialize in my mailbox?

But do I believe it couldn't happen? That somehow you can do anything except find a computer disk?

I told Brian last night on the phone I was tired and sick of worrying so much about all there is to do. And the guy who can't manage to keep his hands off me, the guy who can't follow through on anything says, "Maybe you should stop crying and do something about it." Put on the armor of duty and fake it. Fake it. Fake it.

Okay, Jesus—here it is. It's petty. But you and I both know this is about so much more than a computer disk. With every cell I can muster, I believe it's possible for that disk to show up in my mailbox—the number is on every file on the disk—or to slide out of a shuffle of papers on my desk, or to be in the shallow cardboard box of unclaimed stuff at the helpdesk. It's possible. For an all-powerful God, an all-loving Savior, this is no problem.

And what lesson would there be for me if it didn't turn up? Nothing. A simple kindness from a stranger—checking a disk, returning it to its owner—and I have proof your claims of love for me are true. I even don't need a personal word, just one little action I can count, count as yours.

But with all that power and possibility, if it doesn't show up—it's a choice. It's in your power to give, and I see no reason it's not in your will. "Ask and it will be given to you." You've promised. And dumb as it is, if it doesn't show up, I'll know you've chosen for me doubt and a kind of devastation. Chosen to give it, like a poisoned kiss.

"Brian?"

I could imagine his easy frame standing in the kitchen of his shabby apartment—Stussy t-shirt, carpenter jeans, flat-soled Sketchers—his guitars set in corners like portraits. This was choosing not to hear them anymore.

Sons

"April? Is everything okay?" I didn't usually call in the middle of the day. It was a dingy January afternoon, cold, the clouds slushy and thick. The leaves on the tree out my dorm window were long gone, but today one bird was sitting in one of the inner branches. The room was too hot, outside was too cold. Between us, the bird and I seemed to share a middle place and I looked at it as a companion. It hadn't sung all morning and I suddenly felt like this had to do with me: I was taking its voice, or the bird was giving it.

I wondered how I was going to get through this without giving him the idea it was happening because of who he was. Because that's exactly why it was happening. I'd finally decided to act on things I'd seen in him for years. And there was going to be so much lying to do.

"Brian . . ."

He knew it was coming. His perception finally tuned just when he wouldn't need it anymore. Some kind of divine mockery—breaking up with him just what it took to make him a man I'd stay with.

"How's your day been?" He tried to step away from the quicksand. It had worked before. A casual conversation, an unexpected connection, and I quietly concluded I was just in a phase.

"Brian . . ." I could see him walking toward his bedroom, away from his drunk or videogame-playing roommates, where he'd look around and remember the day we'd painted and arranged the room together. I looked at the picture of us I kept on my desk. We'd been together long enough for me to stop tracking of how many of his shirts I had and for him to run out of room for cards and notes on the edge of his mirror.

I said something about doing a lot of thinking. Something about God. Said a lot of things about being tired of feeling guilty about our physical relationship, about feeling this was the only way to get some control, about being tired of feeling I was the only one who really cared if we screwed up. I talked with my hands even though we were on the phone, pacing, and caught myself in the mirror. I looked tired of a lot of things. Dark swoops under my eyes—layers of exhaustion, like the rings of a tree—from hacking myself to pieces over a 4.0, the idea of a loving Bridegroom, a life full of new people. Tired already of the new secret, the one that couldn't be spoken now because he'd hear it as the reason and it wasn't the reason. Tired after nights of rewriting a British Literature paper.

Then, in the pitch of my tirade on feeling tired and guilty, I glimpsed the bird out the cold window and finally saw through the perpetual fog of guilt and questioning—this was going to be hard. Incremental or accidental as it may have been, I had chosen; and it was like seeing my father choose waving foxtails over food on the table. Over everything I'd been taught, I'd chosen sound—an echoed, hollow cry—over a nest.

The next year, I lived in the past, sealed in dark envelopes of memory reckoning things already history.

On one side, God and questions, on the other, body and experience. Fracturing sides into angles, angles into shapes, I laced lines between parallels. God : body :: question : experience. God : experience :: body : question. I leaned back my whole weight and pulled. Laces winced, things shattered. Some in tiny, tinkling pieces. Some in whopping, woofing thuds.

The year was nights. And memories of nights.

Spinning. Metal platter whirls like an old LP. Kick-kick, pull. Kick-kick, center. Wet fingers slide over juicy clay. Heel of the hand presses in, clay bowls, hollows, the center drying in the friction. Kick-kick, dip. Kick-kick, center.

Brubeck's "Take Five," spinning, toeing round the edge of the empty-dark studio. Kick-kick, *shhhhh*. Clay slip centrifuges off the wheel. Hands dip in the saucy bucket. Pressed between knuckle and thumb, clay rises, balloons, narrows. Kick-kick. Earthy powder dusts the floor; the kick of the foot knocks the dust from the shoes and into the nostrils. Kick-kick, center.

Two, together in a blue hum, a swell of twilight stolen and held while the sky outside has turned black with night. The type of blue where nothing is black or white. The color of bittersweet. The earth is flying around the outer edge of its orbit. On its axis, it has slowed in its rotation just enough. The sun blazes and Saturn spins, but time on earth has stopped. Friction from the slowing warms the bluish glow and everything is quiet. The television and the computer are dormant, the refrigerator upstairs has stopped its drone and the tumbling of the dryer has died with a squawk. No one is up getting a drink of water or letting the dog out.

Take Five. New clay, water palmed from the bucket and smoothed over the ball of earth. Kick-kick, whirl. The letter from Adam. Fort Sill. " . . . I don't have my address yet, but wish I did—that way, I could have people write to me now so that I'd have mail waiting when I got to my battery . . ." People. "Oh well, I'll survive." Kick-kick. " . . . Well, I've got to get going to bed . . .4 a.m . . ." Kick-kick, pull. "Talk to you later! Love, PFC Kauffmann." Later, love. 4 a.m.

I turned off the headlights and hoped the dog wouldn't bark. Adam was still up, he knew I was coming, but the rest of his family was in bed. The house was dark, but the garage door was open and I knocked quietly before going in. I took off my shoes in the entry and quietly voiced his name. He appeared in the doorway to the basement, comfortable. Hazelnut eyes, bronze skin, baritone.

"Hey—how was work?"

He shut off the entry light, leaving the level dark, and I followed him down the stairs. He sat on the arm of the couch and I settled cross-legged in the middle cushions and asked about his day. He'd talked with his commander and the details were settled; he'd be leaving for his second session of training in four days.

We decided what movie to put in and he started it, turned out the lights and sat next to me on the wide sectional. Our arms touched and I could feel his muscle through his shirt, could feel his breathing—listened for it instead of the movie. He asked if I wanted the blanket, I asked if he wanted to share it. I moved closer, he spread it over us. Scenes passed, his arm draped my shoulders, my head found his chest. The movie ended, he pressed the button on the remote and the screen snapped to grey. We watched the glow fade and the house was silent.

In the moment we couldn't see each other something inside relaxed. He whispered, "Can I kiss you?" I turned my face up to him, the arch of my neck a silhouette, but he asked again, "Is that a yes?"

Kick-kick, pull. The question then. Without a pattern. Without a pattern of questions. The first time a statement. "You know what this means." We both knew. Best friend's girlfriend. A secret and a separation. An act that meant choosing to end a first love. A spark on someone else's heap of tinder. An act that gave permission to finally end a first love.

Friday and the radio: the kind of afternoon where the right mix of music throws everything out of proportion. The early January sun warmed the inside of the car and the roads were clear all the way to St. Peter. Christmas still clung to the DJs' chatter. I drove out of the Cities and through the frozen Mississippi river valley toward his college among the farmland of southern Minnesota. Wednesday, Adam had emailed suggesting Brian and I come down to visit for the weekend. I answered that Brian was doing a concert in Illinois [pause] but if he was looking for a visitor, I could come alone.

He answered that I should come if I wanted to.

When I got to Gustavus I met the guys he ran and lifted with and some others in the jazz ensemble. I asked about what they were playing and who belonged with which instrument.

They each seemed to fit them the way Adam fit his baritone sax.

After dinner we went back to his room and decided to settle in for the evening so we'd have the chance to talk a little. His blanket-covered loveseat squatted below the square window and his roommate was out for the evening. We talked about the kind of person Brian was and the good and the difficult accompanying that. When Adam got up to change the CD, I paused and thought, *I'm just tired of trying to explain myself to someone.*

"What?" Adam was facing the stereo putting in *Getz/Gilberto*.

"What do you mean, 'What?'" I asked.

"You were going to say something." He put *The Real Quietstorm* back in its case and scanned for its place on the shelf.

I took a shallow breath and sat staring at the back of his shoulders. "How could you tell I was going to say something?"

He found the CD's place on the shelf and slid it between the other sax players.

"What do you mean how could I tell? April, I can read you like a book."

"Girl from Ipanema" spun out in Gilberto's red-wine Portuguese and Adam walked over to sit back on the couch. "So, what were you going to say?"

Kick-kick, center. The world is the size of the wheel and deep into "Blue Rondo a la Turk," the beat lays back. The saxophone sounds tripping but remains in total control. Maybe my sense of rhythm is weaker than I thought. Two years, two hours. The clay is warm and I gouge my knuckle in and press outward. Two years of tracking—too far? too far? too far? Two hours of talking—how far, how far. The form opens and I press down and out, stressing the center. And if the lines don't matter? If I decide none of the lines matter? The top edge catches, the clay hooks, folds and flies open. It spins splayed and unbalanced. No. Kick-kick, pull. I fold my socks in cotton nuggets because of this. I study literature and my drawer is full of military socks. "Can I kiss you?" "You know what this means." "I'm not looking for a serious relationship right now." "I can read you." I can read you. Read you. This put the slant in my handwriting. "Love, PFC" 4 a.m. This put the slant.

An electricity like blue neon light. I can hear his heart beat through the firm pillow of his chest: for all the jazz of his mind, his body is orchestrated. His heart beats like a well-tuned timpani, his fingers brush the nape of my neck as fingers settling on a violin. I can feel practice calluses on his fingertips. His body is settled in the couch like a stringed bass in its velvet case. Beneath his soft t-shirt fine dark hairs run down his stomach like a set of strings.

We are lying hip to hip in the dark listening to someone upstairs get a glass of water: the peel of the refrigerator seal, the gurgling pour, the smack of the door shutting, footsteps away down the hall. As we listen, his strumming never changes. He lifts his arm and slips it under the back of my shirt and begins to trace his fingers up my spine like a pianist playing scales. I can feel his body changing keys.

The movement we play in is *largo*, measured, in long smooth phrases. I slide my hand inside his sleeve and touch his shoulder, he wraps his arms around my back. We're getting tangled in each other's clothes. His neck smells like myrrh and fallen leaves. I kiss from his ear to his sculpted collarbone and listen for his breathing to deepen. I lift his shirt and kiss down his chest. I lay my head on his stomach and listen for his heart. It's steady, unaffected. I rest my palm on his hip and whisper, "I think I finally figured out how to describe your kisses." When he asks "How?" I can't read his voice. I say, "And I think I'm finally figuring out how to read you." I am lying. Hoping my voice will make the statement true.

I raise myself to look in his eyes. I can see in them that I'm a fool. That I can't resist the hum of his body. He has no plans for a symphony; I know this.

Sons

"Fetching," I say. "Your kisses are fetching." And lean down into a kiss where my burning fuels the cool blue flame.

Kick-kick, pull. Emily. Gaby. Mandy. Jess. Hiroko. Megan. Kick-kick. Emily. Gaby. Mandy. Jess. Hiroko. Megan. Kick-kick, center. "I don't want to be just another name on your list." Just another body. Just a body. Just another body on the list. "April, that will never happen." Emily. Gaby. Mandy. Jess. April. Hiroko. Megan. "Round Midnight" sneaks into the air like blue smoke. Kick-kick, pull.

Take Five. Metal platter turning like an old LP. The clay spins, grows, hollows, sliding between fingers, palms, drying in the cuticles. Kick-kick, pull. Get a love and dirt slides in. Dirt. Dirt slid in so get a love. Letter. "Hello April! Well, I'm down at reception right now. I don't have my address yet, but wish I did—that way, I could have people write to me now so that I'd have mail waiting when I got to my battery. Oh well, I'll survive. Well, I've got to get going to bed. 4:00 is still way too early to get up. I think my circadian rhythms are a little messed up right now. Talk to you later! Love, PFC Kauffmann" Just dirty. ¾ time, edging on too early or too late, spinning, toeing round the edge of the empty, dark studio. But he whispered, "Can I kiss you?" I turned my face up to him, the arch of my neck a silhouette. But he asked again, "Is that a yes?" Kick-kick, *shhhhh*.   *Yes.*

I drifted around the college townhouse in a trail of light switches and door latches trying not to wake the five other girls who would cycle through their morning routines, with various levels of noise, over the next hour and a half. Another alarm went off as I closed the outer door.

I walked down the stairs and across campus in the cold, crunching over the dry shifty snow fallen in the night, the flakes flat and independent like sliding graphite molecules. This time of year, the lampposts would be lit until almost 10 a.m. The grey was thick, heavier the days it didn't snow, but the insulation suited something in me. Mornings were supposed to be quiet—thoughtful—necessary recuperations from the gorging emotional intoxications of the nights. If the noise was too loud or the light too bright too early, I withdrew and walked though the day without latching on. But with a slow, hot shower and breakfast alone, I could float up through the emotional hangover and live my day. Engaging with it was like an accident—like being in a parked car bumped by a passing driver.

Out of habit, or of fear, I kept up my reading. It'd taken me over a year, but I was on the brink of finishing the Bible. Some part of me kept thinking I was missing information—that what I'd been told about Christ and what I knew about the world seemed mismatched because I just didn't have all the facts yet.

After an insulated morning of breakfast and class, I ducked into the prayer chapel to finish the last chapters of Malachi. I'd started reading both Old and New Testament chapters each day, but soon ran out of New Testament and had only prophets left to read. My Bible was paperback and beaten, dirty around the edges from a summer as a camp counselor and smashed in the corners from being banged around in a backpack. This day, I picked it up like it was a book of magic, held it in my flat palms, like somehow when I'd read the last three sections a spring or cog would shift and fragments would tumble down a wall of pegs to land in perfect, sensible order. The heading was promising: The Day of the Lord.

All together the Old Testament had been difficult. The early stories were full of heroes and romance and intrigues, but then came the censuses and laws—not only slow reading but bare, sharp edges. Yahweh claimed to be unchanging, then changed his mind. Jehovah spouted his love for all people then had every child, woman, man, and animal in conquered cities slaughtered. God chose not to consider Job's wife who—because of a cosmic bet over her husband—lost her home and all her children, received no vision, and survived to be rewarded with replacements—consoled, like a mother who's miscarried, that at least she can always have others. And the loving, tender Heavenly Father, who gathers the lost under his wings like a mother hen, commanded that a girl be married to the man who rapes her.

But there was still the chance these final words could right it—could shift the mosaic and lock the tiles into a grand and rational scene.

I read the first two sections too quickly, skimming the words off the page, shaving them up and off like slices of pine from a planer. The chapel seemed supernaturally quiet and dim. I could hear singing from a worship service in the Great Hall, phrases seeping through the walls and hanging in the air like strokes of paint, streaks of sound that hung like they could be walked around. There are others, I thought, a community. Maybe we can make sense of this together, maybe with many feet and hands and minds and hearts churning through the sour curd and thin whey we can find, eventually, we're wading through sweet, nourishing cream. All of us together in the struggle and reward of it.

"And the Lord will turn the hearts of the fathers to their children, and the hearts of the children to their fathers . . ."

It is love—relationship, response, healing, forgiveness. Wounds restored without a scar. Balm. Fresh wind in deep stale valleys. After the hot sun of humanness, so heavy and wet the chambers of the heart strain to expand in it, cool, white-silver nights of glinting disk moons and light-sandaled feet. Harmony. Being alone in wilderness without fear. Being together in light without fear. Awe without violence, compassion without obligation—the citrusy, seeded smell of cracked green leaves, everywhere, free.

" . . . or else." The final words. "Or else I will come and strike the land with a curse."

I began to join my life, through scoffing. On the way to breakfast, a cozy couple holding hands or a pair of women chattering would drive the voice of a reunion-planning type—unwelcome, bounding—into my head: Just think! These are the best days of our lives! I stopped being desolate and started being acrid.

I stopped doing just about everything in my personal life. Instead I sparred with God throughout the days: trapped in a house with a false lover, daring, accusing, and challenging every claim of affection—all the lies from the pulpits, all the Sunday school stories, all the answers to be found in the book of life. Bullshit.

And fool that I was, I'd bought it. Had swallowed it and let the three-pronged, barbed hook rake my faithfully absorbing stomach, my unguarded open valves, the tender flesh of my church-scorned uterus. For too many years I'd lived in doing what I should, dismissing all the evidence it was useless as testing—the stretching and growing of my faith. Believing the problem was with people— that the problem was with me.

And something did lock into place. In stepping back, I saw a perfectly ordered and cruel picture, painted all around with a gold gilded frame. I saw my grandmother marrying in love and my grandfather faithfully leading his family to church while he decided to fuck another woman. I saw my mother proud and strong and pregnant for the first time in slim white overalls showing her mother evidence of a new bridge between them, and being spat at not to wear overalls again because they made her look fat. I saw my father tending God's land and creatures to have them destroyed by God's violence and disease. I saw him gulping down his pride to sustain his father's business and working long hours to support his daughters only to be belittled and accused by his dad, and to miss the steps and play and words that showed his girls' hearts.

And I saw myself, kneeling til my whole legs fell asleep going hollow and dying—praying for the right placement of my heart, for the right kinds of love, for the power to escape my own desire and weakness—until my bones, uncrimping, snapped and popped, handfuls of needles fisting into my thighs and calves. Praying about a stupid, yellow computer disk, and my dreams and hopes for love, and exhaustion at how much trying it took to live in a crumbling, molding world. Trying desperately to do the right thing, as if it mattered, and praying, pleading, as if this Jesus come to woo me actually cared.

Sons

覓

Long, long ago, when the land was cracked and parched, ten suns burned fiercely in the sky. The trees and grass were scorched, and people were dying of thirst in the harshness of the heavens. Then Houyi, a man of uncommon skill, came to court and shot down the suns until only one remained. As his reward, Houyi received an elixir of immortality. He carefully hid the elixir, waiting until he felt worthy to drink it. One day Chang'e, burning with questions and desiring to commune with Houyi, found the elixir and drank it. She began floating up to heaven, but was separated from the man she loved. As she rose, Chang'e grasped the moon, where she lives to this day, both dwelling in the heavens and bound to the earth, met there by sorrow and answers.

The plane rises above the sea mist, the city fading below. In the seats around me, other students are reading, sleeping, talking. After rehearsing mime and script for months we are flying into China to share the gospel. I sit by the window, cross-legged with my shoes on the floor and a thin blanket in my lap—here because I committed to the trip before I found I had no good news to share. There are crumbs of pastry on the tray table and an empty plastic cup glossed with the red emblem of Dragon Air. The last of the misty clouds smears past the window and in the domeless sky, the sun is setting into the clouds, marigold, while the western horizon thins and edges with rose and violet. As we rise, the clouds below become endless, foam on the icy bowl of the sea. In the east, the moon begins to rise. Her sorrowful slopping brow, stroke of nose and purse of mouth are hues of apricot. And she is low, below us as if a reflection in a pond. The cabin lights are off and a few rows back, Ryan clicks on his reading lamp. The cone of yellow light crowns his head and illuminates his pages. His glasses askew, he's absorbing philosophy. The only light in the cabin shines on him. Outside, the moon has risen and she and I gaze at each other through the window. White orb, oval face, yellow cone. Ryan continues to read and as the moon and I mirror each other, she sheds her face and becomes a heavenly body.

"Ready whenever you are, Brooke. We'll just start when you start playing." It's early December and we're polishing the sketches we'll use in China just weeks from now. Brooke adjusts her keyboard and we take places around the mirrored rehearsal room. A floating melody begins and I am alone at center stage. It is my job to be wonderstruck, fascinated by life and representative of humanity in a state of innocence. It is my job to communicate this without words. It is my job to eventually communicate this to an audience on the other side of the world.

I become a child, just wakened—to nature, to consciousness, to life—awed by an imaginary sky, peering under fabricated bushes, chasing a butterfly whose existence is a string of treble notes.

Each time I wheel I see flashes of myself in the mirrored walls—a plain college student in jeans and boots making the spinning clumsy, a foot of brunette hair slipping from its binder, expressions plainer or more exaggerated than I intend. My acting stinks. While being back in drama—working with others, incarnating something—is a welcome distraction from my internal life, it's nearly impossible for me to display a genuine attitude of trust and innocence. I'd have to be able to imagine or believe in one first. But, no one here is evaluating—at least not out loud. None of us are theatre majors and I sense we're in this of nostalgia for high school shows and a justifiable break from academia. The nostalgia, though, can catch me off guard. I've been living between granite slats in my brain as shelter from my flayed emotions, but with certain movements muscle memory will open my pressure-sealed feelings with a sucking pop. Then my annoyed brain chants the commercialized version: Seal is broken when safety button pops up.

The melodic butterfly fades and I turn my capable but underused body to dance. I'm startled by a male figure. The melody takes on minor tones but he coaxes me toward him, beckoning with opened arms and brightened eyes. I take his hand and he sweeps it up so I twirl, twirl. He watches for the relaxation of joy then twists his wrist and I am spun out—hurled by momentum, tossed out tripping onto the floor, palms slapping the tiles, hair flung forward.

"Okay, cut. Let's do that again."

I wind my hair back and Ryan offers me a hand. His fine hair is tousled over his narrow face and slanting cheekbones. He looks like a distractible history professor: almost goofy, except his not-quite-polished bearing only accents the sharpness of his mind.

"You okay?" he asks, genuinely concerned.

"Yeah, fine." His hand is cool as he pulls me up, his fingers precise.

"Can we try something? What if I spin you in instead of around? Here, grab my hand, like this." I take his hand and my boots chirp against the tile as he wraps me into an outfacing embrace. I try to hold my body away from his, standing in my own balance. He smells fantastic. I say, "We could do that," and try to step away, but he holds my hand hard. "Wait—stay here for a minute. Once you're here, relax like you trust me. Then I'll take your other hand—" he reaches for my left hand and my shoulders and thighs settle against the muscles of his lean climber's body. I keep my eyes from the mirrors in front of us. "—and I can throw you out with the other hand." He spins me out, we drop hands before I stop moving.

It's a good change, but affirming his suggestion feels like an admission so I turn to the others. "Brooke, Kevin, what do you think?"

They agree with the change and we decide to quit rehearsal for the night. I take my time gathering my coat and bag, letting people leave, trying to figure out the most casual way to admit I've taken a leap. I walk toward the door, open it, and turn back to say, "Hey Ryan—I picked up tickets to Festival if you're still interested in going on Thursday." I hardly look at him.

"You did? Yeah—"

"Great, I'll see you Thursday then—they're good seats." I rush out the door and down the hall. I didn't look him in the eye, so I have no idea if this is obligation or a date.

My brain wags at this result of one of those ridiculous sucking pops: an unnecessary and unwanted risk, a compromised seal.

A week later, Ryan knocks on my dorm door at 7:30 and we walk the lamp-lit paths across campus to the concert hall. We talk about his friend Sam, his plans for Christmas, his parents. He walks, as usual, hands thrust in pockets, eyes shifting between the path below and the path ahead. A gust of warmth and chatter bursts from the door when we reach the hall. The foyer is decked in evergreen and crimson velvet—garland cascading down the grand staircase, pillars draped in tumbling scarlet, shimmering points of light scattered among the rustle of wool and swell of voices. Inside the hall, clusters of people dot the arcs of seats below and the vaulted ceiling glows like firelight. We find our place and settle into the seats I'd chosen weeks earlier by pacing the balcony of the empty hall, snapping my fingers to find a balance of clack and hollow.

Leaning forward, arm to arm, we look at the program and chat awkwardly until the lights dim. We've spent plenty of time together with the preparations for the trip and the proximity of our tutoring work, but none of it intended.

Finally, color fades from the hall and a white-haired man coughs. Ryan leans back, his knees touching the seat in front of us. A hum begins to vibrate in the center of the dark. Heartbeats slow and deepen and the hum burgeons into a sphere of tenor voices. Ryan closes his eyes, his lashes relaxed on his smooth cheeks, his brows arched and chin raised to meet the music. He listens the way he'd been watching when I'd met him a year ago.

It was dim then too and I'd sat alone toward the back of a local church sanctuary—a curious visitor at a conference on worship and the arts, hoping art would have more to offer than doctrine and experience. An artist at the front of the room painted with full body strokes, the colors on the canvas evidence of a dance as much as a painting. Three rows ahead of me Ryan had watched in the candlelight, enthralled. At the end of the session, he approached the painter. He spoke with hand gestures and listened with his brows turned inward, chin forward, nodding rhythmically. When a sculptor worked next, he watched again, absorbed. His forearms rested on the seat in front of him, his narrow shoulders rising and falling as he breathed. The intensity of his focus burned off etiquette, politic, and self-consciousness like wax fining around a linen wick. The unimportant things—coughing, exit signs, time—became unimportant, slid down the clean edge to pool warm at the bottom. His looking was like oil burning, some flame sucking up fuel from deep inside a clay vessel—light burning, elemental, without smoke. This looking made the world different. It changed, transfigured—made the dance worship, the clay flesh, the strokes art. I had never seen anything. I had looked at Van Gogh, but this seeing put fire in the cypress.

In the dark hall, the sphere of voices constricts, lifts, turns: pulsing ancient and mysterious. *O Come, O Come Immanuel . . . and ransom captive Israel . . .* I watch the music float over Ryan and feel a granite plain in my brain unclamp. . . . *who lies in lonely exile here . . . until the Son of God appear . . .* The plain hovers and slants, tips slowly, smoothly—lists and the melody bursts: *Rejoice! Rejoice! Immanuel shall come to thee, O Israel!*

"All in all, your paper is good—just fix up those citations and go over the other transitions like we did with the first few. It's a research paper, so don't be afraid to tell your reader where you're going." The blonde freshman seems relieved and I hand her a guide sheet for APA citation. She packs up her things.

"And don't let these papers scare you—you're a very clear writer—you have no reason to be intimidated." She says thanks and walks out of the Writing Center, past the two tables and whiteboard that make up the remainder of the tutoring office, and leaves me alone with the duct-tape-hung Christmas lights and purple sketch of Plato's Allegory of the Cave.

I add a fish to the sketched shadows on the cave wall and check the schedule—empty for the rest of the night. I fan a stack of Post-Its on the counter and punch out a couple staples. People are passing in the hallway and the office smells like new textbooks. I wander back to the Writing Center and pull *Tender is the Night* from my bag. Lately I've been drawn to all kinds of worldly, cynical books. They feel like an antidote to the text of fairy tale providence and passion I've spent too much energy trying to believe.

Two chapters into my reading, Ryan walks into the office. He slides his backpack over the shoulders of his button-down until the straps hook on the crooks of his elbows. I see him notice me, and that I'm reading, and he sets piles of books on the table in front of him. One pile for tutoring—western civilizations. One pile for fun—Calvin's commentary on Ephesians and a Greek New Testament. Two weeks ago, after a conversation on finding direction, Ryan left a photocopy of one of Calvin's chapters in my mailbox. His handwritten notes were in the margins, heartfelt jottings mixed with astute philosophical connections.

I manufacture a sigh and put down my book. "Study session tonight?"

"Greek verbs—we spent three hours on Plato yesterday afternoon, so I think most of them have it."

We chat through the doorway.

"Anyone else for you tonight?"

"No more on the schedule, but a few of the profs are requiring a visit and the list is still pretty long. I've started asking how much they're willing to revise before I even read the paper. What verbs?" I push back my chair and walk to his table.

He opens a notebook. "Perfect."

I'm familiar with them, but raise my eyebrows and move closer for the chance to hear him explain. I love that we connect on the intellectual and artistic, and something about his philosophy seems so grounded, rooted, rounded.

"They indicate action completed in the past that has continuing results. Like here—," he opens the Greek New Testament and points, "—the Greek is actually 'you, plural you, *sesōsmenoi*: were saved and continue to experience the results of being saved.'"

He gives other examples and begins to talk about the weakness of English verbs and plurals, spinning the bezel on his watch and gesturing while he speaks. His hair keeps falling in his eyes. I'm about to sit down next to him when a guy in a football cap walks in.

Ryan and I look at him. "CWC or Writing Center?" we ask simultaneously, each of us putting our discipline first.

Football guy grunts, "Paper."

I assume that means me, so I walk around the table and gesture toward the Center. Football guy sits down and as I begin to close the door, Ryan suddenly belts out: "O-oh, say can you see! By the dawn's early light!" He pauses to give me a lopsided grin and continues singing, his muffled voice carrying through the closed door: "Whaa O owd-ee ee ail a uh eye-lie ast eem-een!" I smile back at him through the window. These transitionless juxtapositions are common. For Ryan, there's no great chasm between sacred and secular, mind and heart, body and spirit. As he looks and listens deeply, somehow everything stays whole.

I turn to introduce myself to football guy. Ryan doesn't stop singing until he reaches the land of the free.

The roasted yams, orange inside and starchy, smell sweet and blackened. The woman selling them stands next to a wheeled cart, the yams wrapped in foil, her raven hair short around her almond face. Her lips hardly move as a string of syllables, mumbles and barks, project from them toward the throngs of people passing on the Hong Kong sidewalk. Behind her, buses and truncated cabs honk with reedy horns and people on bikes—men in suits, women in narrow skirts—crank handlebar bells as they pass each other.

We are walking fast—keeping up with the crowd on the sidewalk—but there is so much to look at our troupe of seventeen white faces is stretching into a long line, each of us only looking ahead long enough to be assured (by a blonde head or two in the vicinity) we're not separated. There's something strange about the air—salt, moisture; my Midwestern nose rejects the smell of the sea in the city. Store windows are crowded with posters of Chinese characters, fuchsia and orange, lime and tempera blue; most are puffed and crowded like inflated, squeaking balloons.

The stream of the troupe begins to pool in front of a bus stop and we step into the bus and climb the stairs to sit in the open air. In spite of myself, I notice that Ryan sits with another of the women on the trip. The engine starts and we join the traffic. Bikes and cars continue to stream below us, but most of the city is in the sky. Some of the skyscrapers are cloaked in green mesh from capital to base. Underneath the mesh are stories of latticed bamboo scaffolding. Somehow we find out the buildings wear their shrouds for years; once a skyscraper is finished, the scaffolding stays in place waiting for the building to be remodeled.

We cross a bridge and trees replace the towers of glass and steel. The bus stops and we unload, slinging our backpacks across our shoulders. Ten steps beyond the exhaust, Victoria Harbour winks at the sun. A ribbon of bricks lines the lookout and I walk out to lean on it like a windowsill. Salted air hazes the pewter water and I lean forward, hamstrings and shoulders stretching, into the reflected light. Across the bay, the buildings rise into a wall of shine: silver, copper, crystal, bronze, glass, onyx, pearl.

Under the sleek skyline, chunky, chugging boats weave in the bay. They smell of oil and seaweed and I absorb their tapestry before singling any out of the undulating pewter. The water laps against rusty vessels of green, white, black and red hung with tires and snakes of thick rope. Green and red ferries shuttle across the waves, their insides over-varnished and filled with tin benches. One of the ferries comes close and I can see the back of each bench has a star punched in its center. Something about the benches seems wrong—like a bicycle with unnecessary parts—and I realize the backs flip from one side to the other: they are always sailing forward.

When I get downstairs, Lisa and Kevin are already waiting in the courtyard. It's 7 a.m. in Wuyishan and, with the sun shining, it's warmer outside than in the buildings. Lisa and Kevin are stretching near the door to our breakfast room; their breath rises, white, from their nostrils. I walk toward them in my borrowed running shoes and the odor of hot soymilk hits the back of my throat. A piece from Matthew floats into my brain: And the Son of Man said to them, "Which of you if his child asks for bread, will give him a stone? Or if he asks for a fish, will give him a snake? If you know how to give good gifts to your children, how much more will your Father in heaven give good gifts to those who ask him!" I gag with every sip of soymilk, like trying to swallow a stone.

Lisa and Kevin are morning people, strong bodied and undaunted by physical exertion. Kevin wears shorts and a t-shirt with a stocking cap over his sheared head; he will be sweating in three blocks. Lisa's rusty hair is in a low ponytail, the skin smooth around her lioness eyes. I am wearing too many clothes for running.

Kevin leads the way out of the courtyard and onto the street. Wuyishan is twice the elevation of Minnesota and the air escapes my lungs too quickly. I begin to regret deciding to join them for a run. Both Kevin and Lisa cover the ground in long strides. We pass a field of students doing group exercises in identical nylon suits. We pass an ancient, sinewy tree, its branches spread over hundreds of bicycles. Cloth—laundry in all colors—flutters from the windows and balconies of the student housing, belying the freezing air. Kevin glides around a corner, his calves and biceps pounding like a horse's flanks, and we pass through the gate of our host college. The cold air licks at my cheeks like silk scarves. A group of school boys, in dark and light blue uniforms, spots our white bodies and begins to wave and shout: "Okay!" "Hello!" "Hello!" "Okay!" "Hello!"

I wave and Lisa says, "Hello! Have fun at school!" They beam. All the children we pass shout these same words and the adults turn to each other and talk. We may be the only white people in the city, and I get the idea the Chinese don't exercise individually or on the streets. The elder men and women we pass watch us from small, hooded eyes. Their gaze is something deeper and less shaming than a stare.

Lisa begins to talk—to run a perfectly articulated monologue: "I wonder why they have so many oranges here, you'd think it would be too cold for oranges." She sniffs. "You know what I like about God? He created snot. There's something really great about not just thinking about the idea of snot, but actually making it." I nod at her, breathless and hoping she doesn't ask a question I have to answer through my searing lungs and pounding ears.

"And you know, I'm not really as bothered by the raw food as I thought I'd be—I suppose it helps you can't really tell what's raw and what's not, at least with the seafood, cause it's the same color anyway." I nod. My hair is sliding from its binder, flopping around my shoulders. "I think next time we have fish, I'll try one of the eyeballs—they seem too slimy for chopsticks, but Bryan said they just taste salty. I can't do that rubbery stuff again though—which was it, squid or pig's stomach?" She sniffs again then shouts with a great big smile, "Thanks, Jesus, for snot!"

Another group of boys on the sidewalk ahead thinks she's talking to them and they turn to shout "Hello!" "Hello!" reaching up to catch high-fives as we pass them. Kevin hunches down eye-level with the boys and slaps a line of hands. Lisa bounces and weaves, pivoting like a basketball player and hitting as many hands as she can. I run in a circle around the outside, sympathetic to the ones on the edges.

The boys shout after us all the way down the block—"Hello!" "Okay!" "Okay!" Lisa chatters on about God and mucus—happy at a link that sets me to resentment—and the voices around me go on with their work, nodding and shouting greeting and acquiescence.

"'Jesus replied, 'The kingdom of God does not come with your careful observation.'" Ryan walks in the narrow space between the beds, his olive pants loose around his calves and knees, a black Bible balanced open on his lean, spread fingers. It's easy to imagine him in a narrow clerical robe, pacing a stone room in a German seminary during the Reformation.

The room is a kind of stone, concrete block, and the air is as cold. The furnishings seem appropriate to a cloister: two narrow beds with single coverings and no pillows, bare gritty floor, one high window. I'm layered in a t-shirt, grey long-sleeved shirt and navy fleece. Ryan's layers—t-shirt, collar points—show at the scooped neck of his mottled wool sweater. The only outstanding color in the room is the candy-pink bulge of the bedcover, like a thick layer of frosting on a chunk of cardboard.

Sons

At breakfast, Ryan and I had gotten talking about Van Gogh—a favorite of both of ours—and we carried the conversation back to my temporary room. Jason and a few others rolled their eyes as we left, deeming the conversation contrived and overly erudite, but we discussed in earnest. I was glad for interesting talk to pass the few hours we had until loading in another bus to perform at a church elsewhere in the city. I'd also noticed the scoff of another of the women and counted it as mask to jealousy. Laura and I had begun an unspoken competition for Ryan's attention. As he and I had walked away from the breakfast table, I considered it a victory: they only flirted, but we talked. As soon as we were away from the others, my nastiness and possessiveness faded. Our conversation had tumbled around Van Gogh and his passion for life and his ideas about God and human community, then we'd settled into Ryan's recent thoughts about the idea of the kingdom of God. Now, I watched him pace and read, trying to sort out my feelings as I listened.

"'Nor will people say "Here it is" or "There it is," because the kingdom of God is among you.'" He sits down on the edge of the other bed and leans forward with his elbow on his knee, the book still open on his palm. There is certainly an energy—like some current running along a vein of bedded silver—but I can't tell if it is between us or if we are only standing together on humming ground.

Ryan's eyes are bright with the energy: "And I've been thinking about 'among you' as not just Christ being with them, but as the kingdom of God being among—between—people."

"Which makes sense out of even Jesus praying 'thy kingdom come,'" I say.

"And, explains the parables of the kingdom of God not being 'is where' or 'is when' but 'is like'—because it expresses more of a relationship . . ." He talks quickly, moves closer to the edge of the bed.

"Right—" I say, yanked from my emotional haze by the hook of discovery. I flash though pages of my Bible to scan down the columns: "'The kingdom of heaven is like a man who sowed . . . The kingdom of heaven is like a mustard seed that—'"

Ryan finds the next one in his pages, "'Is like a treasure hidden.'"

I sit up straighter: "'Like a net that was let down into the lake.'"

I see the words, he reads them: "'Like a king who wanted to settle accounts.'"

"'Like a landowner who went out early in the morning.'" He pictures the sunrise.

"'Like a king who prepared for a wedding banquet.'" I picture the prince.

"'Like ten virgins,'" I blush into the open face of the pages, "'who took their lamps and went out to meet the bridegroom.'"

"'Like a man going on a journey.'" He looks straight at me. "See? The kingdom of God between—among people." He swirls his hand between us. "Between us."

Us. The room seems warm. If this is the kingdom of God—between us—I'll take it.

"The kingdom of God between people—anyone," he says, "everyone."

A rock rises from the landscape like the fossilized molar of a giant—smooth-sided, grey, planted by ancients. Unsupported, it thrusts toward the sky, carved with falling lines of red or gold characters, each stroke the width of a human body. The embedded messages have marked sacred places for nineteen generations.

We walk through the octagon gate of the Buddhist monastery—pink admission tickets in hand—and enter a paved courtyard. The white pillars and stairs are carved with red characters, and bonsai trees with bleached, muscular trunks stand at the edges of the covered walkways. Terraced, tiled roofs sit atop the pillars, their corners upturned like the green and red wings of landing birds. Every gate and doorway is marked with red swastikas—an ancient Chinese symbol of luck.

Cami and I walk toward the pagoda in the center of the courtyard, her golden hair and azure eyes drawing looks from the monks and other Chinese tourists in the monastery. A monk in a blue linen tunic and loose pants approaches us and says, "Hello!" a broad smile below his square horn glasses. His hair is short like the other monks' and he projects the soft smoothness of a peach skin.

"American?" he asks, his English clear but over-articulated.

Cami says, "Yes, from Minn-e-so-ta, a *state* in America."

I'm embarrassed by her over articulation, but the monk is undaunted.

He says, "A word, 'insolvable'—you know what it means?"

We try to explain. He doesn't know 'solvable,' so after testing as many synonyms as we find, we resort to metaphor. I start talking about puzzles and he says, "Proverb?"

"Yes! Yes—like a proverb with no answer," I say, struck I am explaining a term of mystery to a Buddhist monk.

He nods vigorously, smiling, eyes shining. Others, Brooke, Kevin and Ryan, join us and the monk says, triumphantly, "I am Bruce!" We all introduce ourselves and Bruce repeats the unfamiliar words. When I say, "April," he lights and says, "Like calendar—you are a month!" We laugh again when he tells Brooke she is little water.

After introductions, Bruce says, "I am learning English—you tell me words?"

Cami jumps in with 'cool,' and 'awesome' and 'cool beans.' I refrain from rolling my eyes; we didn't come all the way across the world for that petty of an exchange. We tell him all these mean something is good. Bruce is eager to add words he knows and says, "Ole sheet!"

Uncertain, we look at each other and he says louder: "*Ole sheet!*"

This time the phrase registers and we gasp—"No, no, no!"

Bruce smiles and says, "From a movie!"

The conversation turns toward Bruce's studies and, somehow, ends with Ryan trying to explain the Virgin Birth. This topic seems to shoot too far—an impossible one for connection—and I'm embarrassed by it until it occurs to me a virgin conceiving is no less complicated than considering myself capable of achieving nirvana.

When it's time to leave, Brooke leaves her own Bible—full of her notes and underlines—with Bruce because he took an interest in the proverbs and was excited about having so many English words at his grasp. I realize I feel proud about it. Not because she's done some kind of evangelizing, but because they've exchanged something and she's given him a gift.

We all say goodbye and wave as we walk over the worn, paved courtyard. Bruce waves back, then gives us two thumbs up and shouts his final greeting, "Cool beans!" the corners of his eyes wrinkled from his wide smile.

It's quiet in the balcony of this dark Asian church. From above, the stage is complete without occupation—the wood planks silent and shadowed in the hiatus between rehearsal and performance. Birds nest in the rafters and their swinging from beam to beam makes this feel like space rather than structure. My bones settle into the wooden bench and I breathe.

We've been traveling and performing for 21 days, most of us have been sick, and there have been three flushing toilets since we left Hong Kong. My last shower was days ago, standing naked in a concrete room, dunking my head to break the crust of ice in the bucket. Cold seared the crown of my head and drops of water pebbled as they hit the floor: eyelids numb, heels frozen to the concrete.

Today, another rehearsal, more changes. While dragging our bodies from another bus to another set of foreign rooms, our leader Dale called another rehearsal. When we got to the church everything was wrong. Dale wanted props, so we hauled fabric and barrels to their places and prepared for the mime dealing with creation, fall, and redemption. Dale sat in the front bench, his fingers stroking his bald forehead, his eyes—the glass one slanted—wild behind his metal frames. In the tenth year he's taken a drama troupe to Asia, he's creating Chinese opera—by now, we're just trying to survive him.

During the rehearsal the swash of black fabric stretched across the stage and Bryan, our tall pre-med with a goatee, began:

"In the beginning . . ." His Adam's apple warbled as he projected the line and he smirked at the over-dramatization. Unseen voices from around the church echoed him. There was scuffling from behind pillars and doorways and planets began to swirl and dodge on stage. In orbit, Lisa watched for stairs and uneven boards and Jason looked for a feasible exit. Ryan pivoted in the center as the sun, grounding the yin of the cycles in a stable yang. Kevin lay flat on his back behind stage to stay out of sight.

"Stop! Stop!"

Dale got up, took Lisa by the shoulders and shoved her to the other side of the stage, shooting air out his nostrils and lumbering across the space to glare at Jason and point at a new spot on the floor. Stashed behind a pillar, I muttered for the thousandth time that we're taking direction from a man with no depth perception. Kevin, the last of us to get frustrated, sighed. We have rehearsed this mime for six months. We have never done the same thing twice. Watching, I shook my head: unpolished, unorganized, vulgar—so much for communicating anything sacred.

Now, in the silent balcony, Ryan is napping on a bench three rows in front of me. We came here separately. He walked in and laid down; we didn't acknowledge each other directly. When he stirs I can hear the sighing of his jacket.

I can hear the rhythm of his breathing, just on the edge of a snore. I wonder what he is dreaming about and when I'll get him for another conversation. He's begun spending more time with Laura and I'm jealous of the attention.

Looking past the place he's lying and up into the rafters, I think there must be something to be said for people who seek refuge in the same places. The birds swing back up into their nest, settling in as a pair, and I think: why else would we both be here?

"But does idealized love contribute to spiritual growth?"

The room is a ray of sunshine. The books we've traded throughout the trip are scattered on the narrow bed of Ryan's temporary room, awash in lemon light: Dostoyevsky, a collection of Martin Luther King Jr.'s sermons, Henri Nouwen's exploration of Rembrandt's *Return of the Prodigal Son*. They cast cornered shadows on the ripples in the sheets. Ryan is standing against the wall, his ankles crossed, palms against the wood, fingers fluttering. His body moves with his mind. I've been sitting on the bed, cross-legged, since entering his room.

"I think it does," I answer.

"How though?" He seems skeptical.

"Well, not idealized love like, whatever you want it to be, but idealized in the real sense—what it really is—the pure kernel of the thing." I'm talking to the top of his head. His fingers flutter against the wall again and he nods in thought. I'm not sure he's convinced.

"But, what love is is different to people—" he says.

"But the idealizing—the mental part—isn't that alone a kind of contemplation? If you're thinking about what love could be aren't you somehow growing?"

I can't tell if I'm trying to impress him, or justifying my current perspective on life, or if I'm simply desperate to be on the subject of love with him—however it comes about.

Ryan pushes away from the wall and takes a few steps along the edge of the bed. His khakis swish against the sheet. The floor creaks as he thinks.

"Maybe, but useful growth?"

"Hard growth." I re-cross my legs and scoot back to lean against part of the metal frame. "Hard because the more you realize the ideal of a thing, the more you see its absence."

He gestures toward the book on the bed, "But that's the whole Grand Inquisitor thing—"

"—that eventually you have to act on the absence."

Ryan sits on the bed and twirls the bezel on his watch. In the citrus light I can see the smudges on his glasses.

"But, I don't think that's the point—" he says. "Dostoevsky is always about the human side of things." He picks up *The Brothers Karamazov* and flips through the pages toward something in his mind.

"Like *Crime and Punishment*—Raskolnikov can't live in his theory."

"Right." He stops at a place in the book. "Here:' . . . the kiss glows in his heart, but the old man adheres to his idea . . .' The kiss, the experience is what glows—despite the accusations and ideas. The inquisitor is lost because he holds on to the idea instead of the experience."

I nod and pretend to think, smooth a corner of the sheet and look at the light feathered over it. My response doesn't need any germination, it's the slab I've been living with for a year:

"But the inquisitor believes what he believes based on experience—he began believing there was love and good, but experience itself proved otherwise."

Ryan answers nonchalantly, as if this were just a conversation:

"But, eventually he decides to accept one experience over the other. Even after he receives a kiss from Christ himself, it's not enough for him. Apparently, nothing would be enough."

Our rusted ferry roars up to the dock, exhaust fumes blowing back into the cabin and stinging our tired eyes. On the shore, a knot of Chinese villagers stare at the boat. The island, the water, and the villagers' clothing are all the same grey. Their dark faces and lacquered eyes anchor the grey. They're calling us missionaries. They're saying we're the first white missionaries to ever visit this village. The women hold their infants close and look at us like we're ghosts—elongated, bleached and bloodless creatures, glowing against the grey they inhabit.

When we step off the boat, an elderly man, his face round and spotted beneath his cap, lights a string of firecrackers and holds the end as the cluster of powder packets bursts toward his hand. Without a glance, he flips his wrist just before the last explodes and the final cracker pops in the air. He leads us from the dock, lighting and tossing firecrackers, and the women follow at a distance behind us. At the edge of the village a group of men are standing with instruments—a trumpet, a snare drum, a trombone, cymbals. They are dressed like a marching band in old Salvation Army suits. When we meet them, they begin to play, making a parade of us and the trail of villagers. The cymbals clash as we walk past piles of chipped bricks and buildings without glass in the windows. On the side of the chalky road, a woman stands in front of a large frame weaving invisible thread onto its pegs with a long stick. A mound of pilled and grainy cotton sits on the woodpile beside her.

The band leads us to the door of the church and stops playing. Three firecrackers burst. We look at each other, uncertain what to do. A woman steps out and takes the arm of Lisa's coat to lead her inside.

The air in the church is as cold as the concrete walls and a few bare bulbs hang from the ceiling. The woman beckons us to the front where other women begin to hand us bowls of soup—two for each of us—the dishes chipped and mismatched. There's a table with oranges and peanuts laid out and a row of glasses with tea leaves floating in them. The villagers' feet scuff on the concrete as they come in and sit on the wooden benches. They have been waiting for us and now sit to watch us consume their gifts. We are late, so the thick, black soup is cold and the tea stings the sides of our tongues like alcohol. We can hardly swallow this feast of the village treasures.

When we are finished eating, we perform here, though exhausted. We pull out unfelt energies because we're ashamed. We are battered by brief endurance of our audience's lifetime burdens. And at the end of the night, they surround us—like the warm experience of fire—giving and glowing.

Months after China, Ryan and I ran into each other outside the pottery studio in a basement hallway of the college. He'd just returned from a semester in the Oregon mountains studying philosophy; I was preparing for a semester of literature in England. His face was bronzed, his glasses smeared. He played with the straps on his backpack as we talked. I suggested we have dinner in the dining center sometime to talk about his trip: "I'd love to hear about it, get the names of the books you're reading—hear what you're pondering these days." I told him to call me sometime if he found he had a free night. He looked at the floor, scuffed a foot, and said, "Yeah."

Sons

The next time I saw him, he'd come to my campus apartment to watch television with Laura, who'd ended up, unchosen, as one of my roommates. They watched *Friends* and teased each other. When she walked to the kitchen for another glass of water, she joked with him: "Not sure you can you live without me for a minute." He looked at her, laughed, and said, "Nope."

Sunlight pours down the vaulted stones, flows along the black earth and stirs the air to rising, up, through the smooth green leaves, among the barkless branches blooming with smooth green leaves, up, up, along the wedges and towers of rock, up, between the clinging, knuckled pines, to hover as a weightless river. The valley steeps in tea.

On the floor of the valley, a curve of young people walk single file. The line of their bodies, a blue stroke, turns back on itself, winds and eddies. The valley is silent. Their line crosses and curves into a crease in the vaulted stone.

Heads are bowed as the bodies rise. The line turns jagged and fragmented along the face of the vaulted rock. A figure at the end of the line stops to drink and gazes across the valley.

As the figures ascend behind a finger of stone, the dash of blue shrinks against the rock until the last figure vanishes between shaking bamboo leaves. The figures appear again, higher, the stone face below them falling away into the valley like a waterfall. Their line bends toward the valley then away into the mountains.

There, the figures rise from a crevice and step from the vegetation to find six robed men, heads shaved. The men invite them to sit on low stools before a table of ancient tree trunk, gnarled and polished. The oldest man passes a loop of beads through his fingers. His hands are brown and wrinkled. Brittle leaves are cracked into steaming water and offered. Steam curls from the cups, up, while a girl watches the pale silhouette of the rising moon. Ascends, up, while, because she is here, the girl looks, longs, and considers afresh the placement of heavenly bodies.

"April..."

I could see the indigo shades and shadows on the smooth skin of Betsy's face, the rest of her wrapped up against the Minnesota February night: a crinkly ski jacket, a white knitted scarf that glowed onto her chin and cheeks, her willowy fingers resting on the steering wheel. Her planner on the console between us now marked with things I wouldn't hear about anymore.

"April, I need to hear what you're feeling . . ." She talked to me while I stared into the windshield from the passenger's seat. The evening was clearer than any had been since I'd returned from China. The van was getting colder as the heat slipped between the metal door frames and slid out the icy glass. Soon the cycle would reverse and the cold would seep inside. The moon was somewhere full and silver, but the light in the van seemed artificial, like we sat in the hollow of a flashing TV set flickering in an empty room.

I wondered how I was going to get through this without deciding it was happening because of who I was—without concluding in the midst of some prayer or writing this was punishment and more evidence that, instead of dwelling among humble frames for heaven, I was living in a gilded hell. And, there was going to be so much lying to do.

"April..."

Somehow I knew it was coming. The sheer soap opera logic of it was bound to make things come together this way. Some kind of divine mockery. Dating Brian was just what it took to make him the kind of man my best friend would love.

I said something about being thrilled, about thinking—and who would know better than me? —they were a great match. Something about God. Said a lot about being glad, if I'd had to work hard at a relationship, at least any good to come of it would be going to my best friend. I talked with my hands laid on my lap, looking between them and Betsy's tentatively relaxing face. Heaven knew I'd been looking at a lot of things other than her or Brian lately—stitching myself from hacked pieces into some person with whole thoughts about bodies and divine love, plans and happenstance, a life full of new people. I may have even said something about that. What I didn't say was waiting until I left the country to start dating the first man I'd loved was cheap and shadowy, a betrayal from my closest friend.

Instead, I revved further into a glossy-grinned cheer, acting bigger and bigger with a chuckle about the irony of it and a dismissive wave about guessing I deserved something like this after all. It *had* been a year since the breakup, and I'd *always* known it was just a matter of time before the two of them got together. Between intentional eye contact and a chorus of 'it's fine—it is fine because it will be fine,' I glimpsed the moonlight on one of the bare branches and felt a triangle lock down. This one would be forever. And no matter how okay it became, the two people I'd been most intimate with had chosen the thin impressions they had of each other over the deepest things I'd had to offer. This was like being divorced by a sister, watching her choose to lose you, her best friend.

And looking out the windshield at the bare moonlit branches I knew fighting up from this, choosing not to close back down to granite brain and spiteful Christ, was going to be hard. Harder than anything, because I'd have to choose it—not regardless—but in denial of my experience.

I am here by none of my own doing. I have done nothing to get to this place.

An overnight bus ride. Trying to sleep with my head ducked in a carpeted cabinet to have dark and quiet, waking with my heart flabby. Then sitting up to the front window, heart sloshing, hanging over the driver on the top of a double-decker bus. Out the window: tender, growing, pink-topped hills, the sunrise like a settling pashmina. Rose, lavender, sage, buttercup. Each color every color. And tender grapevines reaching across the fields, leaves like children's hands, tendrils like a child's finger, reaching, reaching for a small warm touch of assurance.

There are three things too amazing for me, four I do not understand: a flowered meadow, silence, Easter, and loneliness. In the midst of four months studying literature abroad, I have ended up at a monastery in Burgundy, spending a week in silence in the days before Easter. It's been raining for three months: England. And now I wake up in pink sun over hazy lavender and yellow flax fields and visit a chapel full of flame. I eat crusty bread with sweet butter and skim the skin from bowls of dusky hot chocolate. I drink lemony tea in the afternoon, my reflection quivering in the amber scooped from a hot silver tub. I sleep alone in a barrack room, on a top bunk, with other women in their twenties and in silence in rooms around me. I pray, in common, in chant, three times a day. It's the only sound I make. I walk in the afternoons past white cows with stout horns and wet noses in green fields. I eat with women from Holland, Germany, Canada, and Spain without speaking—passing and seasoning simple meals without words. I paint with a child's box of watercolors, spongy swamps of pigment and a plastic brush, whatever flowers I find. I don't ask why I do any of it. It's here, and I am, and that seems reason enough.

This morning I woke in my rocking metal bed to the monastery bells and went to shower in a common bathroom. There are eleven of us women here in silence and other young people all around the monastery, meeting each other and talking about faith. Our home while we are silent is a square of barracks around open grass with a common room on one side and a bathroom on the other. They all have steel corrugated roofs and concrete floors.

Clutching my toothbrush, toothpaste, towel, and soap, I walked across the open grass, the hem of my pants lapped by dew. As I brushed in front of the chipped and murky mirror, two other women came and prepared to bathe, balancing their towels on hooks and shower rods and checking the curtains for spiders and webs. I stepped in a shower after them and undressed, hanging my clothes carefully in backward order with my puny hand towel balanced on top like a wig.

In succession, each of us flipped on the water with the fill-and-burst spray of uncovered pipes. Three loud consecutive commands for quiet: Shh. Shh. Shh. I sucked my naked body back against the wall, pressing my lungs up and pulling my hips back. The cold water spattered on the skin of my stomach. I flipped my hand in and out of the stream waiting for the heat. The backs of my legs hovered near the cold concrete. Flip: Wait. Flip: Wait. I think we simultaneously gave up.

One by one, the sound of the water splashing on the floor deadened as our bodies broke the flow. Icy water smeared my shoulders, breasts, and hips, and slathered my stomach and thighs. Novocain cold streamed down my scalp. Cells chilled. Air thrust from my lungs.

Lined up in a monastery bathroom, we gasped and puffed: a line of dignified, seeking women slotted in shower stalls. Together we sucked air and uttered little cries of shock, no one covering the experience with words. With only the whimpering presence of body, we panted and chuckled, together in our freezing flesh.

This place is all mornings. Even on the way to evening prayer, the bells clang and peel, tumbling up and out like a sunrise even as the sky is beginning to settle and smolder. I walk alone from our barracks onto the noisy gravel path. By now the others here know by sight who's in silence, and I can move in a bubble of solitude even in the crowd. The permission in silence is astounding. I am allowed to watch and absorb without responding or entertaining. I'm basking in the relief of this release.

I walk to the left entrance of the chapel—a low, plain building without stone or a steeple—and drag my fingers across the bushes by the door. The leaves pass their aroma and make my hands smell of dust and rosemary. The smell itself is like a ritual, accessible but rooted in something ancient and mysterious. Rosemary, for remembrance, and dust.

The inside of the chapel is dark and open. Thin green carpet covers the ground and skinny steel pillars hold up the ceiling. Down the center, two rows of boxes form an aisle. The boxes are planted with the rosemary-smelling bushes. Bach is playing. Across the room four stained glass windows punch color into the dim. They are square and monochromatic like four lit jewels set in the wall: blue, red, green, orange. The front of the chapel blazes. Triangles of orange fabric leap to the ceiling and open squares of clay stack and scatter across the floor like burning coals. The candles in them flicker. Together they ripple and pulse.

I find my spot on the floor next to the bushes, close enough to the front all I can see is the flame. I sit large to preserve my space as others walk in and settle. I cannot open when surrounded. I hate that the practical things make such a difference, and am disappointed.

I slide off my shoes, pulling the back strap over my calloused heel, and sit hugging my knees staring at the cratered soles and cracked leather waiting for them to transfigure into a spiritual lesson. The only one that comes to mind I've heard before. The brothers walk in and I hear the rustle of their white robes as they kneel in the aisle. Bach stops and there's a pause while the hidden musicians prepare to begin the service. I keep staring at my shoes. I know there's a digital sign in the left corner, its red numbers showing the location of the first song. It's so practical. I hate it—when I don't need it.

The songs begin: simple repeated chants in all the languages of the world. The sound seems to come from everywhere, blooming out of the air above my head and glowing there. A haunted line breathes low through the flute and something in my guts stretches down and pools. It's time to begin my prayer.

I turn my legs and kneel on the thin carpet, dirt poking into the skin on my knees and forearms, my forehead resting in my palms. I try to pray in silence, directing words at God from the back of my bowed skull. I feel my knees and palms and elbows. I can smell my own breath. I see an hourglass of dark between my knees and hanging breasts. My hair is spilled on the gritty floor around my head. The chants continue to float above me, a cantor breaking through like a message-bearer, his tenor voice open like a bell.

Sons

I fold my knuckles and lay my forehead on the ground to try and mouth my prayer. "God—. Lord—" Neither of these are right. "El Roi." It feels strange to shape the Hebrew words, artificial, appropriated. *The God who sees me.* I feel my legs and toes begin to tingle. They'll be numb soon and standing will be clenching and difficult. Songs continue to open in the air. A man reads in French from one of the gospels. The chapel is silent. The silence rings in its emptiness. Full of bodies and candles and dirt. Rings in its openness. Full of body and sandals and hurt. "El Roi." *El Roi*. This uses all my faith, is my entire prayer.

I spend my afternoons in the meadow enclosed by our barracks. It's full of perfect weeds: white puff dandelions, yellow buttercups, tall tiny daisies. I sit with my back against an adolescent poplar—slender and strong as a young girl—or laying in the grasses looking through their green hollow and fibery stems floating with white and yellow orbs. I feel like a small bird from here, hidden, with my big, glassy eyes. I think I could be content to eat seeds.

All afternoon I read and write. I've made a new journal of cheap paper, stitched together with a sewing kit and covered with one of my simple watercolor flowers. I write rambling entries, dreaming about marriage and motherhood, open to femininity and hope uncut by intellectualism and practicality. I blow dandelion seeds and make wishes. For the first time in my life I write without embarrassment about the softness of the air on my skin and the feeling of my hips when I walk. For the first time I think it might be worth it to be a woman. For the first time 'bride' sloughs its puny, girlish pettiness and becomes regal, self-possessed, and crowned. For the first time, I think lovingly about the word 'daughter' and the music of 'Our Father who art in heaven.'

Each morning Sister Anne stands with us in the common room and gives us scripture for the day. She wears simple wool skirts, flat brown sandals, and blouses with pockets. She speaks to us in English, reading from the gospels or of Jonah or Deborah with her head uncovered—speaking like these men and women were her family, saying 'Jesus' with her soft French accent (*jsah-see*) easily, like he is among her friends. I picture over and over again the women at the tomb and keep thinking her name is Mary. She is so much like one, in wisdom and peace, who's finished crying.

We don't speak among ourselves except to translate. Esther takes in the English and in quiet intercessions speaks to one of the other women in Spanish. Esther reminds me of the other Mary, somehow both young and wise.

Sometimes Sister Anne reads the scripture in French as she knows it, letting each of us find our way to the text in our own language.

"Jean, chapitre vingt et un, verset vingt-cinq: Jésus a accompli encore bien d'autres choses. Si on voulait les raconter une à une, je pense que le monde entier ne suffirait pas pour contenir tous les livres qu'il faudrait écrire."

Esther whispers, "Jesús hizo muchas otras cosas también. Si cada de una fueran escritas, me imagino que aún el mundo entero no tendría espacio para los libros que serían escritos."

Later today I stood among tables of the pottery the brothers make to support their community. Each piece has a small stamp on the bottom, TAIZÉ, because none of them take personal credit for the work they do. I stood before the cash register with a wide-bowled oil lamp in my hands—its purchase both a recognition I would have to leave this place and a weak, material effort to carry away a piece of its flame. I was trying to buy a symbol.

As I waited, I thought of the scripture Sister Anne had given us: a library in heaven. I stood with the clay lamp in my hands, elbows akimbo, passport pouch across my shoulders, and a scene dropped into my head. A young man with dark skin and wavy hair stood in front of a shelf full of books. Young, the Son of God was sliding one book back onto the shelf, smiling—sliding back onto the shelf one of my books, smiling. *I have books in God's library.* I stood in line for the cash register, my arms full of clay, lashes laced in blinking tears.

Sons

Today is Maundy Thursday, a day named for washing feet—one of the days before. I have never been able to feel guilty or joyful enough for Easter—have always felt less like a believer this time of the year than ever. So I try to ignore it, even here. Especially here. Where expectation for miracle, for magic, for transcendence is so easy. Maundy Thursday, Good Friday, Holy Week. The labels bring back my skepticism, my intellectualizing, my nuancing. My oh-so-sophisticated realism. The core becomes a hard gunmetal marble, a flint, a scrutinizing mirror.

During afternoon prayer I analyze the parts of the service, categorize the ecumenical whole into traceable influences from denominations, countries, orders, and hemispheres. The icon on the cross from the Russians, robes from the Benedictines, urgent social intercessories from the liberation theologians, thin green carpet from the Americans. I pray as I should: dignified, orderly, focused on the articulatable needs of others. "Be with Megan and Mindy as they are deciding what to do with their lives." "Be with Mom and Dad as they prepare to have an empty house." "Be with Betsy and Brian as they grow in their relationship." After climbing the stairs of personal petition, I reach a higher plateau blooming with words and diction. "Be with all those suffering: the mothers trying to care for their children, the children without food or protection, all of those living in wars." I begin to walk around the plateau, harvesting the waving pre-assembled bouquets. "Burden the powerful with mercy and the powerless with strength. Grant sustaining beauty to refugees and exiles. Free prisoners from unjust jailers and use just jailers to free prisoners from themselves. Heal the sick and wounded, both in body and in spirit. Provide balm for the abandoned and the lonely. Shine wisdom on the leaders and infuse their actions with grace." I have no trouble filling the hour.

After prayer, I sling on my shoes and duck out of the chapel. The sun stamps my retina, slams into the back of my eyes. My pupils wince and squeeze. Insects buzz in the brightness, humming over the rosemary-smelling bushes. The feet of those in front of me munch on the gravel as they move toward their tents in knots of three or four, walking like philosophers leaving the Akademeia. I walk along the road thinking of how much I accomplished during prayer. The insects keep buzzing.

I leave the main road, crossing through the low, snapping gate marking the area for those in silence, and look especially into the bush of orange pompoms in front of the sisters' quarters. The bugs are so loud today I guess they've gathered between the branches. I walk around the sisters' house toward the entrance to the meadow and turn the corner toward the line with our shower towels rocking in the breeze.

There are no bugs. A man is mowing down my meadow.

A riding lawn mower is circling the square, rolling over the dandelions, slicing the buttercups. Clouds of dandelion seeds rock in the air around the mower.

They are mowing my meadow. They are mowing my meadow.

The rasping of the motors files the inside of my ears. The buttercups bend forward as the mower rolls over them, clump limp behind the blade. The exhaust spits more rocking seeds into the air.

No.

I feel like I'm shivering. The man gets off his mower and rakes up the stripe behind it. He scoops up the flowers and dumps them in a black trash bag.

No.

There's an open spot in the top of my head, a space left when something small and hard evaporated.

Jesus, stop them. Jesus, please stop them.

The man gets back on the mower and continues cutting. Another man rides into the meadow from the back corner by the shower. They shout to each other in French, one pointing to a pocket in the corner of the square, the other nodding and gesturing he'll cut around the poplar.

Someone has kicked me in the chest, a foot punching my sternum inches into my lungs.

They are cutting my buttercups. They are throwing away my wishes.

The second man finishes clearing the far corner. The first man is still circling, putting edges on the meadow and shrinking the wild, growing space. He's turning the meadow into an English lawn. I feel like my blood is draining out the bottoms of my feet.

Jesus, stop them. Jesus, please stop them.

The second man rides up next to the first. They talk, the first nods at something the other has said then jumps off the mower and rakes up the new stripe behind him while the other man leaves. What's left will be no trouble for one mower.

Clutching the slouching black bag, the man gets back on the mower. He swings the wheel wide to slice through the middle of the square, but instead of looping, he keeps going.

Without looking back, he rides off to the corner, leaving the job unfinished.

I stand staring at the square of flowers in front of me. A banner of dandelion seeds trails, rocking, to the ground.

Thank you. Thank you.

A young woman, feeling foreign here in so many ways, moves among the flowers stooping and gathering in plain khaki shorts and a white t-shirt. She's not old enough for her movements to be poised or precise, but she's past the teenage awkwardness of arms and legs moving in visible intention. She's young and a woman: her body is as noticeable to others, slim and taut, and as transparent to herself, unpained and unmanaged, as it will ever be.

She walks carefully through the patch, picking buttercups with her right hand and placing their thin stems in her left, holding them openly in a ring of her thumb and finger, their bowing heads brushing the tan skin at the base of her thumb and the curl of her knuckle. The very tip of her tongue has snuck out the right corner of her lips. It's difficult to tell if this is a genuine slip into unselfconsciousness or a plotted action to move her mind toward a certain childlikeness.

Her long brown hair is wound at the back of her head absorbing the sun as she picks only the best blooms, careful not to leave any single spot bare. Finally, she steps high over the grass and walks into a common room to wrap the bottoms of the stems in cool wet paper, a brown speckled swaddling to rest in her palm.

She leaves the common room and the square and walks down the road toward the chapel, her sandals scuffing the gravel, the flowers carefully unremarkable at her left side. They are a private gift.

Inside the chapel she finds her place and kneels on the gritty floor, her forehead in her palms, the flowers on the thin carpet in front of her shoulder. She drops into prayer like a contraction—single-minded, her spirit laboring and unspooling like a ribbon pulling from her chest out her throat. She prays water, sunlight, comfort, and armor, pushing them from her chest, laboring to birth them, against gravity, from the muscles of her heart. She prays until her spirit is so tired she weeps.

When she's finished, her eyes are wet and her breathing is settled. She wipes the clinging water from her eyelashes and sits. In the aisle, between the bushes, others are gathered around a cross laying in the center. She sees them from a distance as people kneeling around a piece of painted wood, medieval and superstitious. She feels foolish, but determines to give her gift anyway, tired of letting self-consciousness and practicality close every window.

Stepping quietly, she walks to the cross and kneels behind the people around it. Candles flicker at the head and feet and at the tip of each nailed hand, casting a sheen on the lacquer. Having grown up in a church without images, she doesn't know how to look at this cross with a face. But she understands symbol. She holds the buttercups in her hands and bends her body forward, her mind full of space after the emptying of her prayer. She's not used to giving things like this, so she only opens her hands and lets the flowers to the floor while she marks the gift in herself with a wordless sort of space, an open sphere of acknowledgement. The flowers lay by his right open hand.

She sits up again, looking down at her shadow from the candlelight, sand pressing in her knees and tired, and an unthought phrase opens in her. *I'll take them with me.* She smiles in the candlelight, in disbelief or wonder. Maybe both.

That night while she's trying to express her experience, she writes—feeling foolish and humble and honest—"I just wanted to give him something for his kitchen table."

HOLY GHOSTS

Heaps of flakes have been falling all night, an epoch of snow, like an infinite hourglass of sky turned to mark the night in a long and separate time. I sit in a foamy chair in the dorm lounge, everything inside—the empty fireplace, clattery room, square lights—weird against the full and falling air out the window. Feet of snow are flooding the door wells and sidewalks—lofty piles rise against the sides of buildings, a shifting, gathering filling, turning landscape into container. Weather is slowly displacing, filling up instead of falling down, and still the air is lush with flakes.

 Häns lies with his body back over the pool table, knees bent over the edge, sandy blonde head resting on his palms between angled elbows. The raised edge of the table thrusts his hips up, brings a slightly scandalous attention to them. Bodied compact and solid, his muscled arm stretches his grey t-shirt as he moves one hand from behind his head and taps his fingers on his stomach as we talk. An old friend from high school, he came to campus to visit his best friends. We ran into each other in the cafeteria and chatted a little to catch up. Snow started falling, and we kept talking.

 Touring the lounge—shifting from couch to counter-side stools to window sills—we've talked the world around. He's asked what God has been teaching me lately and I've asked about the important things he's learned since leaving our hometown high school; we've both shared thoughts on the relationships we've had and the things we've learned about ourselves, good and bad, from having them.

 Now, at 3:30 in the morning, the snow and Häns are shocking: familiar grounds now in totally different atmosphere. At dinner, I had plans, too much homework, laundry. Now I sit in a lounge at

3:30 in the morning, talking to someone I already know and I just keep looking at him. Stunned. I like the unpremeditated way he moves his body, the way we share turf. Even as he lies across the pool table, rocking his ankles as he talks about the relationship he is just ending, I feel the substance of our relationship building, gathering up. Not like tension, the wicking pull of a tight string, but like the compression keeping bridges straight, in solid lines, pressed by outside sources.

At 3:30 in the morning, the sky is falling and I am thinking I might be in love with someone I've always known. It's like a riverbed suddenly filled. Everything around is solid, stable: I know his family, we've gone to the same church, we are sitting in the most unexotic context possible. Monday night, Baptist college, too tired to even scope for dates. Then, a change in weather, the banks brim, and with nothing destroyed everything is in motion. He's not a best friend, a blind date, or even a first sight, but this is simply something I never expected.

"But I guess God just reveals it to you when it's time, doesn't he?" Häns swivels his eyes toward mine, talking half to himself about his recent breakup. For the last hour we've been set like counselor and counseled: me sitting up and nodding, him lying back and talking.

I've never felt especially like anything was revealed to me—the way some people stand in the grocery store and let the Spirit lead them toward the right loaf of bread—but the shifts of this night have got me rethinking spiritual intervention. Häns showed up, when I wasn't looking for anyone to show up, to visit my college the night of the biggest snowfall in years. But the most shocking thing, strangely enough, is the calm. Like something ethereal has kissed the place in the back of my lungs always so busy fluttering over relationships—an unnatural, tangible sort of peace has inserted itself, not just around me, but into me.

Häns rolls sideways and props his head on an elbow while the rough fingers of his other hand start to brush the felt.

"Like how we ran into each other tonight—it's like I just needed to talk to you and God led me to come visit Troy and

Michael and led you to go eat dinner at the same time. Like it was just meant to be."

I think he's getting cocky—can tell I'm seeing him in some new way. Not that he doesn't mean it. Häns has would never make light of God, but I think he's noticed I've been looking at more than his eyes.

In another strange intervention, I'm not even bothered if he has. So many of the relationships I've had with men, with God, have been based on such ideals, fantasies, ideas—fixations on the past or future, denials of spoken reality, divisions of soul from body. But this could be real—a relationship with both substance and meaning, truth and presence. Finally some mixture of body and thought and faith all in one place instead of fractured and segmented.

Häns sits up and checks his watch, the cuffs of his pants jangling around his ankles. He says he should probably get back to the guys' dorm so he doesn't come in too late. His cheeks bunch up as he smiles; Troy and Michael are infamous for midnight espresso. But I stand up and we move toward our coats and the door. It's late—he's only got three hours before he needs to be back at his drafting job—and ending this night doesn't seem a great loss. I'm strangely certain we'll be seeing a lot of each other.

We hug goodbye and Häns puts on his loose jacket and says he'll call tomorrow. He pushes out the door and lopes through the knee-high snow, then turns back to wave. I wave back and turn to walk to my place.

As the snow pushes my shins, I wonder if this feeling is what people mean when they talk about the presence of the Holy Spirit. I've always been suspicious of the part of God so easily confused with my own thoughts, feelings, and hormones; but, the best I can think right now is something about this relationship feels anointed. I never could have manufactured this—haven't even thought Häns' name in more than a year. If this is some kind of intervention, it's powerful enough to work against all my natural guards and fears, powerful enough to orchestrate whole lives—weather, hormones, the whole of the physical world—by simple infusion.

Back in my dark apartment, I get ready for bed on some kind of edge. I'm excited, but keep looking at the corners of the mirror as I brush my teeth and feel uncomfortable as I undress—suddenly uncertain how much of my world, how much of my body, are actually mine.

Three and a half years later, on a May morning, Häns and I step into the silver shell of Charles DeGaulle Airport to begin a week in Paris.

Our marriage is two years old and since our wedding I've finished my degree, started a fulltime journalism job, and begun grad school. Häns has quit his corporate drafting job and taken his tradesman's hands to the university to begin a program in design. We're poor but I scrounged freelance jobs writing music reviews and theologically-reductive articles on evolution for an evangelical teen website. It was worth it: we needed a vacation.

I'd surprised Häns with the gift two weeks before we embarked. We sat at a veneered table in an American-chain Chinese restaurant—the kind where the smell of oil is the smell of the food—and I pushed a red plastic takeout box toward him. The box was covered with white ribbon curls and stuffed with tinsel and he raised a sandy eyebrow at it. He pulled a fortune cookie out of the box and turned it over, then turned on his high-pitched, cartoon voice and tapped the cookie on the edge of the tray like an egg: "Vhat do vee have here?" He was just like a cartoon squirrel with those big eyes and rounded cheeks. It was part of what I'd fallen for—around him I could laugh without feeling I was being irresponsible. When we'd cracked open the cookie, I found he couldn't read the French. Though he'd been studying the language, he didn't comprehend the fortune I'd planted. I was disproportionately disappointed. I'd thought I had a clear understanding of his strengths, and that he was more perceptive.

In the airport, milky light washes the high trusses and stainless baggage carousels, and time seems diffused. My swollen feet feel thick under my laces as we shift fleece sweaters and passport pouches along with the other passengers, adjusting to the morning and the opportunity to stand. The flight was long, but more pleasant with someone to sleep on, and customs went more smoothly than I expected.

Now, it's hard to tell if Häns is awed or just tired. He's usually such a big reactor I'm beginning to be bothered. I'd expected him to talk so much about the trip I'd get sick of the idea. I figured the airport—passport stamps, announcements in French, exchange to Euros—would loose the excitement in my husband, who had never been overseas. Maybe he's just overwhelmed.

We watch the bright packs and black suitcases progress past our fellow passengers, most of whom seem to be arriving home. Women with silk scarves click up the handles on their wheeled bags and clacked away across the terrazzo to catch cabs. The crowd shrinks and Häns and I drift toward another young sweatshirted and camera-slung couple we'd seen on the plane. The four of us seem to be wearing too much color. Soon we're the only people, besides a couple letting their quiet three-year-old walk along the carousel, watching one unclaimed bag circle on the snaking track.

I begin scanning for an information desk and we start a traveler's conversation: Waiting too? Where you from? Think we should be worried about the bags? They're backpacking, just married, spending the month: honeymooners. Their olive and black packs finally slide down the ramp and they buckle in. Have fun, good luck.

"I don't think of backpacking as the ideal honeymoon situation," I say.

Häns nods.

"I guess I think of a little more luxury—and privacy—for . . . that."

The silver track turns its repetitive circle. We watch the one suitcase glide past. I look at the floor and think, *Not that it would have mattered for us.* Our honeymoon had been anything but a sex-fest. After waiting until we were married, living on conviction and confidence, we'd assumed our self-control would be blessed with success in the marriage bed. Two years later, we're still waiting for any kind of blessing.

The track repeats its monotonous circle. We sit on the terrazzo and I consider that asking about our missing belongings will be more of a hassle than just continuing to wait. We chew granola bars and watch the track crawl. The airport seems too quiet.

Häns and I sit on the edge of the plaza fountain tearing chunks off a baguette and swiping them in foil-wrapped wedges of white cheese. Across the Seine, the steeple of Notre Dame stares back over the *quai* and the smell of river water drifts into the plaza. A tooth-cratered apple rests in my left palm and we each sip *jus de raisins* from boxes with straws. The clock on the Hôtel de Ville reads eleven twenty-five and *le Tricolore* folds and furls in the quiet breeze. Pigeons warble and scatter, pompous as musketeers, around the iron plaza lamps and flop themselves onto the heads of the pediment statues. The morning has been quiet, insulated by the clouds, and we chew and watch the pigeons. The cheese is unbelievably good.

Mostly we sit and look at things and absorb the sun when it drops through. I keep watching Häns—checking to see if he's enjoying himself—and I think the pressure is getting to us both. There are few things less satisfying than the event that must be enjoyed.

At the patisserie this morning I made him order, pushing him to use his French: a simple statement of address, desire and thanks. We received what we were hoping to get, paid correctly, and the clerk counted the change back in French without giving any special attention. By my estimation a successful encounter. But Häns had seemed shaken and insecure for the rest of the morning. We were both tired after the luggage fiasco, details of finding our small hotel and the jetlag, but the disconnection between us is something more than exhaustion and something less than a fight. So far, the City of Light isn't shedding any light on that.

We finish eating, and I tuck the empty drink boxes into the backpack. Both of us sit waiting for the other to stand up. Häns is comfortable enough in his drawstring cargos and zip-up fleece—his shoulder leaning against a concrete pillar. It's early enough in the day I can still smell the sharpness of his cologne against the mellow odor of water. I'm sitting with both feet on the ground, the strap of the camera bag slung across my narrow torso.

"So."

"Yeah."

We watch a mottled pigeon strut toward us. Neither of us wants to be the one to bring in the 'What now?', but if it has to be said, we both want to ask first to avoid being the one who has to answer. It's a round we've been skirting for years now: who will be the first to say something is wrong and who will be the one who has to answer?

I pull out the guidebook and flip through it to justify the dead space. He watches a man walk diagonally across the plaza.

"Well, what do you want to do for the rest of the day?" I ask.

"What do you want to show me? I'm really fine with whatever. We can just figure out where to go now and take the rest from there."

This is always his answer: to just do the next thing and see what comes after. I want to find out where the end is and work up to it. I don't know how to talk about this in terms of being, so he thinks I've become a high-strung over-planner. It's not an argument I'm in the mood to try and articulate today.

Somehow we decide to walk down Boulevard Saint Michel to the Luxembourg Gardens to read for a while and figure out the rest of the day. As we walk, my Michelin map in hand, I mentally tick off the sites we'll now have to backtrack to see: Pont Neuf and the river vendors, Notre Dame, Delunay's Saint Severin, the Pantheon.

In the gardens, we walk over the gravel, through the chestnut grove, and pick two chairs next to the lawn in front of the Sénat building. A row of lacy rosebushes, blooms pink and ruffled, divides the lawn and the crunchy white gravel and as we sit it becomes pleasant to have no idea if it's the city's lunch hour, rush hour, or holiday. We unload our bags and Häns pulls out his vintage, leather-bound copy of *The Vicomte de Bragelonne*. The pages are tissue-thin and edged in gold next to the burgundy cover. This is the fourth in Dumas' musketeers series from a set I found in

Stratford-Upon-Avon while studying abroad. After four months overseas during our engagement, I carefully wrapped the five books in paper and brought them home for Häns as a wedding gift: "Dearest Häns, May the imagination and valor in these pages find a place to dwell in your heart. With deepest love, April." Soon after our vows, I found out he needed the wish. Beneath his verbal confidence, deep-rooted insecurity and self-doubt made him D'Artagnan's foil.

I take out my journal and try to write a little, thinking about children and Hemingway, but the jetlag is still too much. Häns flips his fragile pages and I doze in the green metal chair.

"We have to go."

"What?" Häns is startled hearing imperatives from the wife he thought was sleeping. He sits up and lets his book fall to his lap.

"Do you have any Advil? Tylenol—" I can feel the pain beginning to roll in. Like a thunderstorm, it's full and creeping. When it breaks, my muscles will flash and flood, hardly breathing between strikes. A stupid, predictable pain—monthly—but deep, and even now filling my mouth with the shallow metal of nausea. It's a pain physically debilitating—one forcing me to show the vulnerability and neediness I hate, to acknowledge my incapacity to overcome my body—all made worse by its puny, feminine cause.

I see Häns' eyes flash around the square—he doesn't have anything—no friendly matron around to ask—and the words?

"Can you walk?"

"I think so, still. Let's go quick—"

Häns scoops up our things and dumps them in his bag. He throws my bag over his shoulder and takes my arm to help me up: "Come on babe . . . it's okay . . . we'll get you back to the room . . . you can lay down—I'll read to you if you want . . . it's gonna be okay . . ."

A flash of sweat slaps my skin, my stomach lurches. Two more steps and I'm going to burst—vomit—I have to sit down. "I have to sit down."

Häns guides me to a bench in the grove and I curl my knees to my chin. Breathe. Just breathe. Just think about breathing. Don't throw up. Don't throw up. Don't think about throwing up.

My muscles roil, pulling, pulling, pulling—a hard, glistening knot. A strike of sweat flashes again. The noise leaks out my throat, *Uhuuuu . . .* The taste of metal is dripping down the insides of my teeth. I can hardly lock onto what Häns is saying.

"I'll be back. I'll be right back. It's gonna be okay—"

The storm is full, rolling tighter, tighter, pushing on itself until my bones are worthless and the hard knot is the center, structure, substance. The spaces my mind can grasp are filled with words:

Stupid, stupid, worthless pain. Not death, not cancer, not life. Don't throw up, don't think about throwing up. Breathe. Breathe. Not even hunger, not torture. Not birthing anything. Just look at the ground, the steady, even gravel. Unjustifiable. Unjustifiable center of the world—don't pull me in here for nothing—don't pull me into myself for nothing. Unproductive, meaningless pain. Pain for nothing.

I am panting: scared to be noticed, scared not to be noticed. Trying not to think about this as something God does to women. The metal drops to my stomach then springs back to my tongue. The knot is pushing, rushing, so much a part of myself I can't even curse it.

The thunder pauses, recoils for a moment and I breathe, trying to put my body into a sleep-state—to trick my muscles back under the control of my mind. I close my eyes and decide when the storm rolls back I'll embrace it: bask in it like sunshine and diffuse it though absorption. My skin is cold and wet.

Clench, crescendo. Dull racing sucking into a center. Stupid pain, stupid, worthless pain. From the body. From the choice. From my body. From—I throw open my nerves and walk full into it.

Gather it in, spread it over. Put on the purple cloak. Enter the black cave. Naked. Touchable. Push the knot open. *Uhuuuu . . .* Let it in. Choose to feel it everywhere. Choose to feel it.

Feet crunch over the gravel and I'm terrified someone is coming to help me. Breathe, breathe. Be ready to appear fine—not ashy, not thundering. The pain constricts. The knot pulls tight again.

"April, April. Baby, it's okay. I'm sorry I was so long. Here—take these. Take these. I have water."

Häns' hair is ruffled back and he breathes like he's been running. His eyes are wild. My mouth is dripping with copper. He tears a box in half to get it open and pops two white pills out of their plastic bubbles.

"How did you?" I ask, panting with my mouth spread open.

"Never mind—here, baby—I have water. Take these."

I strap all my consciousness to making my stomach accept the pills. Häns rubs the palm of his hand on my back. One: swallow. Two: swallow. Sip. Don't throw up. Don't heave it back out before it can help. I breathe through my teeth. Choose to be overrun.

"It's okay, baby—it's gonna be okay now."

I focus on feeling his hand sweep across my shoulders. Brush. brush. I try to feel his heart beat through his fingertips. Brush. Brush. Try to let his body, comfort, enter.

"Babe—wake up, we fell asleep."

My contacts scratch my eyeballs. The hotel room is dim. The fourth day of our trip and we haven't shaken the jetlag. Behind Häns the paned window is thrown open next to the rose printed curtains. The white enamel on the sill and edges glows in the peach and tan sunset. I sit up and blink, my legs heavy on top of the comforter. Outside the window, roofs float out like barges on a hazy ocean. The small TV hanging from the plastered ceiling is on. It ruins the light in the rest of the room.

"TV?" TV in Paris? He's letting me sleep in Paris while he watches TV?

"I just flipped it on. Here—" Häns clicks it off and comes to stand by the side of the bed. One of his cheeks still has a faint wrinkle pressed into it. "We should probably find something to eat."

Holy Ghosts

Häns helps me out of bed and I stand by the window and put drops in my eyes to smooth the sandpaper. Singular sounds come to the window from the street. One car passing on the narrow alley, the clicking of shoes, a man's voice asking where to stack crates of greens.

We gather our passports and lock the room with its skeleton key. We walk down the curved switchback stair, past the tiny lobby and breakfast room, and out of our narrow hotel into the street. Around the corner, singular images drift around the courtyard: small white lights wound into vines and awnings, worn paving stones, tended trees with gathered branches perched over benches, a woman with a knee-length red coat walking her dog diagonally through the square.

We tuck into an uncovered table with a friendly waitress who delivers chopsticks and soy sauce. It's probably silly to eat Asian food in Paris and we'll probably pay too much for it here, but the square is paced to our tired rhythm and we recognize more of the words on this menu. I begin to wake up and the dusky quiet of the courtyard dissipates my crabbiness. All the props are in place. Dinner in Paris = a kind and attentive husband, a twinkling courtyard, dusk, two glasses of rosé wine. The clichés alone are convincing.

Our waitress brings a steaming dish of Asian barbequed chicken, surely an insulting mismatch to our wine, but the sun is setting and the world is beginning to shrink to the size of our perfect table. Neither of us anymore care if we look like clumsy tourists. We're getting drunk on the atmosphere and it feels like this night might finally be what we came to Paris for.

Dishes and glasses clink around us and, sitting in Van Gogh's rich and glowing café, we talk about all the places we'd like to go in the world. I ask lots of questions and love his answering between drinks with his mouth full. His enjoyment is so unconcealed, so palpable—a permission to forget what this costs, how soon it will be over, and all the shades of responsibility. We're young. Life is good.

And, we could make love tonight.

I sink the thought, trying to keep a secret from my analytical self, and nibble a little more food.

"So, Madame, what do you want to do with our evening?" Häns asks, laying his napkin on the table and leaning forward on his elbows. His eyes are shiny in the café light.

I pick up my wine glass, swirling the pink pool around the glossy bowl. "Well, Monsieur, we could go walk by the Seine, or see the Eiffel Tower, or," I take a sip and look at him over the top of my glass, "we could just go back to our room."

His eyes widen and for a second his face is full of little boy eagerness. I try not to see the desperation in it. Then he sits back and swirls his glass in a cigar and cognac pose. He begins with the matching text, "Well, I'm sure the Seine is lovely this evening—" then meets my eyes and sets down his glass. His shoulders become loose and authentic. "Come on, babe, let me take you home."

We walk away from the café, my arm linked in the crook of his elbow. We fit: exactly the right height for each other, his shoulder at exactly the right place for me to rest my temple. He's strong, I'm slender, our evenings are full of intellectual conversation: the perfect couple. He steers us around the block and we walk with matching steps past darkened bakeries and antique print shops. At the hotel, he opens the door and the man at the front desk nods as we pass. Upstairs, the stage is set: small hotel room in Paris (shabby but clean), violet light from the open window, covered bed upstage center. Häns and I climb the zigzagging stairs, the old wood creaking beneath the dusty carpet. "I'm really glad to be here with you, April," he says. I squeeze his muscled arm and put my head back on his shoulder as he pulls the room key from his pocket and turns the lock.

Keys jingle and a door swings open upstage center.

Me. (*Aware of walking through a threshold, holding his arm.*) I'm glad to be here with you too, Häns.

Häns closes and locks the door.

Me. (*Looking out the window, trying to keep a connection with the mood outside.*) Let's leave the lights off.

HÄNS walks to the window, wraps his arms around me and begins kissing the back of my neck. The kisses are tender and nuzzling. I keep my eyes open and look at the sky, mentally repeating the context: Paris, sunset, husband. Häns slides around to kiss me on the lips.

WIFE. (*Shutting eyes and tilting chin upward, between kisses.*) I love you, baby.

HÄNS. (*Stops, looks in her eyes.*) I love you, April.

The two kiss by the window, her hands sliding around his back, open like antennae trying to catch the right frequency.

VIXEN. (*Pushes forward to kiss him hard, steers him backward toward the bed then gives his shoulders a shove so he tumbles onto it. Smiling.*) Now I've got you.

HÄNS. (*Arms sprawled out, smiling.*) I guess you do.

VIXEN pounces on top and kisses his neck and shoulders, sits up and flings off her shirt. He sits up and pulls his shirt over muscular shoulders, grabs her, unhooks her bra and pulls her back down onto the bed.

HÄNS. (*Breathless, smiling.*) I love when your hair falls around me.

VIXEN. (*Pushing her breast and shoulder to his lips.*) Kiss me.

Häns puts his hand on her back and rolls her onto the comforter, leaning over her and kissing her skin.

APRIL. (*Vulnerable, grasping.*) I need to see your eyes. Let me see your eyes.

Häns lifts his head and she clutches him to her.

APRIL. (*Clinging, looking wide-eyed at the ceiling.*) Talk to me. Let me hear your voice.

HÄNS. It's okay, baby, I'm right here. Everything's going to be all right.

APRIL. But what if it's not? What if it's never all right? What if it's always—

HÄNS. (*Cradling her, speaking into her ear.*) Shh . . . it's okay, April. Let's just try. Just try to relax.

WIFE. (*Detached, looking at the ceiling.*) Yeah.

The two rearrange themselves on the bed, moving pillows. The room has been getting darker and is now nearly black. Their two figures move as shadows. There's the sound of clothing being dropped off the side of the bed and voices.

SHE. Wait. Here.

HE. I love you baby. I love you so much.

SHE. (*A tight intake of breath, a slow round exhale.*)

HE. (*Whispering.*) I love you.

Silence.

SHE. (*Sharp inhale.*) No. Stop—stop.

HE. A different way? We could try it a different way.

The sound of sniffling, her figure crawls away to the edge of the bed.

SHE. (*Crying.*) I'm sorry, baby . . . I'm sorry . . .

HE. (*Reaching out to touch her shoulder.*) Shh . . . it's okay.

SHE. If you need to go and . . . Go.

HE. No, I'm here with you.

The stage is dark and silent except for the sound of her choppy breathing. She faces the window curled in a tight ball. He rubs her shoulder from across the bed. The stage darkens further. The actors silently, separately, plead with the phantom director. As it's been for years, there's no intervention, no accompaniment—no indication of any response.

The house is white, two stories, with windows big enough to let in whole quilts of light. After Versailles, this seems manageable—like the 18th century Parisian equivalent of a split level. Modest. Modest wrought iron fences, modest formal gardens. One fountain and bare polished floors. A house full of modest marble sculptures.

I was not in love with Rodin when we got here. This is not what I was looking for.

There is no swirling, seething passion, no vibrancy. The house is white, the gardens are green, the sculptures are still. They sit. Like owls. Like doves. Like lessons. Needing nothing from you. In need of nothing. Like patience.

Holy Ghosts

I don't know how to look at sculpture: this doesn't jar or offend me, doesn't make a narrative, doesn't shout symbols. Häns and I walk around the house, with its modest number of visitors, and I'm alarmed only by this: the closest kin to the feeling these sculptures give me is annoyance. They don't have to do anything, they're just here. And even when I try, I can't get to the tipping point of flare and resolution. They're like a hum in the house you can't find the source of.

We're two separate people today. I don't check he sees before I cross the creaking wood floor to another room. We don't discuss the art or read the placards to each other.

The Kiss, the flashy sculpture, is a nation away in the Tate with other flashy artwork. Rodin's house is full of pieces: hands, feet, parts of faces. Small women, like dolls, and a plain old man. The strapping sons and daughters have left for more exotic places. The ones still in the house are those that don't require worship. I'm afraid to think where Häns and I would be displayed, in which permanent collection we'd belong.

In the garden, Häns and I take pictures of each other posing in front of a replica of *The Thinker*. I mock bewilderment. Häns mocks confusion. It's the most emotion we display all afternoon. As I press the shutter I think: these pictures are for people back home—images of a fairy tale, evidence our trip really was all they dream theirs could be. This is what the experience of our marriage has been. Evidence. Of something.

Versailles at least was a great big fake—that was the point. We'd gotten the point and could fall asleep on the train ride back with some sense of completion. St. Chappelle had had no point for us to begin with—it was an accidental discovery—so its simple existence was justification enough. This place, though—where we'd planned to come—this place of humming statues: why were we here? Why was I here?

We buy *glacé* from a cart in the garden and sit at the far end of the lawn licking the soft peach and coconut mounds. The taste is so subtle the cones are like sugared cardboard. I wonder if they were made in America.

Across the stretch of green I look in the arched windows and scan the outdoor pieces. Nowhere can you catch their eyes. But the hands are understandable—in pieces or on bodies, Rodin put his own hands in their hands: a clenched fist, an open palm, four curled fingers, a cradled grasp. It suddenly seems every other part of the sculptures exists only to justify the hands. So much work for such a small thing.

I look over at Häns' hands, rough, his fingers weft. I call him my builder—a name for the root and pinnacle of his future profession—but we both mean it bigger. His hands are the hands to hold the soft heads of my babies, the hands for caressing, for drawing forms that mean light, worship, learning, and comfort. Are they supposed to justify all the other parts of this structure? Are they what is justified? These hands I love may never be able to touch me. Is something wrong with me? Is something wrong with them? Did God put his own hands in these hands?

We return home as we'd left it: unsatisfied, unanswered.

Then, it started raining.

The skin on my palms is peeling, separating from the creases like riverbanks sheering from a canyon. I scrape away the whitish peels, my palm flinching, and clear the dead, moist skin from my fingernails. My grandmother says the same thing happened to her when she met my grandfather.

All night I hover above sleep unable to grasp the black raven as it swoops just below.

"It's just like the recycling thing—how many times do I have to ask you what we have to do to get the milk jugs from the counter to the bin?"

"So now this is about recycling?"

"No!"

"You just can't let go of anything, can you, April? The recycling?"

"It's an example, Häns—an example! Every time we try to talk about something you get hung up on the details—"

"*I* get hung up on the details?"

"Will you let me *finish*?"

"'Every time *I* get hung up on the details.'"

"It's like you're incapable of seeing past the examples—"

"Then maybe you should just tell me what the issue is."

"What the issue is? You've got to be kidding me—you know what the issue is."

"Enlighten me."

"Whatever you leave undone needs to be finished. While you walk around telling me to relax—to stop worrying about *every*thing—to just trust God things will turn out—*I'm* the one running around picking up the pieces!"

The bathroom is black and hard. I sit on the floor with the bones of my spine against the door. The sides of my eyeballs are numb, like black has been injected there. A waxy dim coats the window.

Holy Ghosts

This year is not the first for anything. Not the first year married, not the first year in the house, or the job, or finished with school. It's an old t-shirt pulled from the dryer; comfortable, but only because I've been in it before, and worn to tearing.

"You treat me like a child, April—like I'm someone to be controlled and disciplined, like I'm just this bomb of irresponsibility waiting to destroy your perfect, organized world. You respond to me like I'm a two-year-old."

He's sitting on the edge of the loveseat after pacing the room, his body like a raccoon's, uncertain of offense or defense, capable of damage, incapable of guile.

The sun is setting on our anger. It's orange and hovering. Wan and weak. I'm standing at the edge of the room, staring at the pictures on the wall, only acknowledging him from the corner of my eye. The stripes from the blinds lay across my body and over the carpet.

A thin green cloud seeps over my shoulder and down across the stripes. I open my mouth:

"Well?"

He hates my planning. Because it eliminates him.
I hate his dreaming. Because it requires me.

All afternoon at work I sit in my grey cubicle and chew the inside of my cheek and bite my finger with my molars. Just to try to stay awake.

Three envelopes in the mail today. Bill. Bill. White security paper lined with black spittle, like the inside is covered with ants. Plastic window on the front, thin, black and blue logo in the corner. Bounced check.

"I was thinking maybe we could go to church in the morning."

"Go ahead if you want," I say, daring him to choose God over me. Daring him to make something more important than our problems.

He sets the alarm for the service, the clean creases of his knuckles strong in the lamplight. "You can decide in the morning if you want to come."

He hits snooze for an hour, his fingers flopping toward the button. I lie awake looking at the ceiling.

Thanksgiving: working. I sit and talk with a homeless man between taking pictures of the celebrity volunteers. He, tired and dignified, says: Every morning when I wake up, I start thanking God for everything I touch. With my eyes closed I thank him for the bed I'm sleeping in. Then I open my eyes and thank him for my sight. When I stand, I thank him for my legs. At the sink, I thank him for my toothbrush, for warm water, for this stocking cap I put on. That's how I keep going.

I can tell this is true because he speaks not like a manicured housewife about her Zantac but like a diabetic about his insulin. Because this has nothing to do with quality of life, it has to do with surviving.

He asks me if I'm going to try to take his picture for a brochure and when I get to leave to have dinner with my family.

Mom calls today, just to check in. They had babies by this point in their marriage. Bigger things to think about. Distractions. And at least enough sex to make three babies.

Out my bedroom window, the maple's branches droop like tired fingers. It's early and the grey sky lacks the light to be pearlescent. The air is weighted. Three wood ducks land behind the maple and I'm finding it hard to breathe.

Holy Ghosts

"I just don't understand. It's like my switch won't trip—like now I suddenly have a switch and I don't know where it is."

We're sitting in the car in the dark. For once I'm in the driver's seat. We're both facing forward. He's been in the studio for 18 hours. I'll take him back again in 5 and he won't come home at all tomorrow night.

"I always thought our physical life would be my safe place—my free place—one place where I wasn't even capable of planning or worrying or measuring. Because it used to be."

He lets the silence sit while we both add words: Used to be with . . .

"I just don't understand what's different now, now that there's no reason to resist. I refuse to believe the 'forbidden fruit' thing is the whole answer—that the only reason I could be magnetized before was because sex wasn't allowed. Even if that was it, all the guilt I tortured myself with about 'going too far' would have been more than enough to defuse it. I just don't know what's changed."

As soon as I say it, an answer precipitates from the saturated air. The seed locks and the dark crystal stacks layers, sucking in all the floating grains of guilt and question and exhaustion, racing out like ice binding up a black window: He's the difference, he's the problem.

I don't mean it, I don't believe it, but we freeze in the crystal, one more ringing guess to try and thaw.

***

Driving home tonight, after an evening with old friends back from Alaska, Colorado, nearly all the lights were green. Even with all the people in the city the streets were open and the intersections empty. Van Morrison on the radio. I looked at the stars through the top curve of the windshield between flashes from the passing streetlights. The last stoplight red, I pulled into the driveway just as the next song ended in "home . . . where I want to be. Home . . . where I want to be."

Walking inside, locking the door, I found Häns asleep sitting on the couch under the light of two lamps. I said his name and touched his knee, still in my coat and shoes, and he blinked and asked me how he got there.

I don't know, baby, how did we get here?

Read about Ophelia today. And Dido. Starting to think of the timelessness of literature in a different way. And what it means to believe love and possession share a dimension.

"Maybe tomorrow we could maybe try to spend a little time together?"

My hands are full of shampoo, he puts one hand on my back and rubs my shoulder with the other, looking in my eyes. His shoulder gets dappled with the beads of warm water and they slide down his landscaped arm. His body feels warm and stable; I feel a glimmer.

"Yeah, that would be nice," I say, looking him back in the eyes. "I miss you."

I mean it.

Dear God, whatever it takes—romance, wine, goofiness, time, distraction, rushing, faking, hoping, ignoring, dressing, dancing, reading, insomnia, weariness, rain, wind, sun, moon—whatever it takes, make it happen. Please, make it happen. Whatever it takes.

Everything is wrong. Mint makes his mouth cold. Blankets make me too warm. I'm tense. He fumbles. There's a way to end it. It means giving up on something. I swallow hard.

And Daphne. What if you want to be rescued without running?

After work today I park, pull the emergency brake, and realize I don't remember any of the drive home. Not a sound, not an image.

Betsy and I sit in Heidi's living room planted in a secondhand sectional. Heidi clomps in from the kitchen in the enormous wedge sandals she wears to reach five feet and clacks a bowl of salsa on the table. She raises her hand like a grade-schooler. Betsy and I stop our conversation and nod at her.

"Sorry. But, do you like my new haircut?" She takes out her clips and shakes her blonde layers down over the shoulders of her Ralph Lauren peasant shirt.

"Very cute."

"Okay—go on." She plops down next to Betsy's composed frame. "So, things are good?"

Betsy leans forward and pinches a chip. She breaks off a corner and nods. For all her modesty, she's practically fluttering. She and Brian are newlyweds.

"Sometimes I'm not really as interested as he is, but I know it's important to be selfless," she pops off another corner of the chip, "You know, to be a good wife to him."

"So you're his sex slave," Heidi jokes.

"Heidi!" Betsy blushes. "No! But you know what I mean, it's biblical: the whole "The wife's body does not belong to her alone, but also to her husband" thing."

"And—" Heidi interjects, munching a tomato-drenched chip, "You get to jump him whenever you want, too."

Betsy smiles and shakes her head, "I think it's really more an issue for me, to recognize his needs and how they're more important." She chews the chip corner. "And, I always end up feeling good about it in the end."

Heidi reaches for another scoop of salsa and teases, "So basically, you like being a sex slave."

I sit on the tattered fabric and watch them giggle.

We try again. After, I smile and turn over to fall asleep. When I hear his breathing settle, I creep through the dark to the bathroom and sob.

There's a small spider in the corner of the bathroom floor. She's slender and industrious, her thin legs step across her web polishing and fastening. The web is empty, nothing caught to struggle or die, nothing grotesque. She's simply housekeeping. As she is, her satisfaction costs nothing. I watch her weaving in the dusty corner over the dull grey linoleum. Even I, in all my spitefulness, couldn't bring myself to crush her. There'd be no reason for it.

Sex is supposed to be a symbol for the union of Christ with the church, the mystical intermingling, the binding spirit. I guess God makes the same mistake: chancing ruin, risking metaphor across worlds.

We're talking around the d-words. Both of them.

"I have rearranged myself around you—let go, loosened up—given up my preferences for predictability, solitude, control. And some of it has been good—real growth. But I am tired of bending my entire self, I'm tired of it, Häns."

"Well, I'm sorry that you've had to change your life while I've sat here doing nothing."

The whole room darkens. The aperture in my eyes closes down: click. click. But nothing gets sharper, only darker.

"never mind"

"What?"

"Never mind."

I slide on my shoes and pivot toward the door. Everything moves slowly. "This isn't working, Häns." The keys spill over the edge of the counter and clatter on the end of the chain.

"Where are you going? April, where are you going?"

"I don't know." I click the door shut behind me.

I drive. Sit in parking lots. Finally crawl in the backseat and lie with the seatbelt buckles stabbing into my kidney. Afraid of being found, afraid of being raped. The car gets hot, so hot, and the sky stays dark.

Betsy calls me at Heidi's. She's heard I'm there for dinner, probably staying the night. I know they've talked before I get the phone. Heidi says, "Stay as long as you need to." Betsy says, "I just don't think it's right."

"Please come home."
"I'm just not ready."

Back home I ask Häns to move his hunting rifle or its ammunition. To put it somewhere I can't find it.

Today I saw it in another closet. Not even covered, the clip and shells where they've always been.

Häns and I see a counselor. She decides I have generalized anxiety and he has attention deficit disorder. We spend most the time trying to convince her we have a valid issue, that it's not just archaic Judeo-Christian fundamentalist guilt-based repression.

He is kissing. His eyes are closed, his forehead smooth, his neck tilted back for mine tilted forward. His hair is always darker in the winter. He breathes in my ear and kisses my neck. His hand plants on my chest. I curve my shoulder to move away. He drops his hand and keeps kissing, his eyes closed, his lips trying to push forward.
    I sidle out of the nook of the couch, out from under his body and stand for a minute in the murky five o'clock light. We don't look at each other. I walk to the bathroom and lock the door.
    Sit and stare at the tub.
    The floor creaks outside.
    "April, what are you doing?"

    "What are you doing?"

"Crying! *Just* crying."

The house is silent.

"Baby, please come out. I can help you to bed. I'll sleep on the couch."

I stare at the tub.

I stare at the tub.

Blood. Chemicals. He'd have insurance money, could finish school. Could find someone else, better. Knives in the kitchen, quiet. My mom, sisters. Pain. Botching it. Could go quiet to the kitchen.

I wait for him to fall asleep. Stare into the dark.

At four I wake in the watery grey. Turn the handle to leave the bathroom. He's spread on the floor in front of the door, sleeping. His presence holding me in.

This is your fault. Your fault.

My palms are peeling again: my grandparents' legacy. The ones who got divorced because of an affair.

But it's cold enough I don't flinch scraping the dead off anymore. I don't really feel it.

In the car, driving to work or to pick up Häns from studio, I listen to the same songs on repeat. The drive between the house and the U is just long enough for me to pry back the round, steel door to my emotions, stare at the water below until it begins to well, feel like I still could cry, then close it and walk away before Häns comes down the long stairs of the College of Architecture and opens the car door. It's always the radio on when he climbs in.

Holy Ghosts

On the drive today the trees are bare and the snow is old. It's the week before Christmas and the glisten and shimmer has been stirred into a sandy corpse left to decompose by the side of the residential roads. There's no stillness, no wind, and no definition in the sky. The bump of the railroad tracks is hardly jarring. This is the time of year when nothing is noticeable and I'm hardly capable of noticing.

Into the dirty canvas of my days fall dark drops of heavy red—rusty—both from fresh cuts and partially coagulated. When I begin to think color no longer exists, we fight, and the fabric of marriage shows black and white except, from persimmon to vermillion, all shades of hurt. I can no longer even Technicolor the days, fake as that was.

The 1950s houses creep closer to the street as I near the city and the trees shrink and recede to alleys with telephone poles. I'm staring in my well, waiting for the sight of the pool to sink in, but the flow of motion inside requires movement outside. A stoplight slams the trap door shut. The flatness around me is cold.

At green, the song switches and I shift through the gears into a mummified tunnel vision. Brown slush, road, motion. I weave through the streets, park, and walk diagonally through lots. The grey metal of the city gazes past the windy crosswalk in the sourceless light of four o' clock sunsets. The sun is far away these months, traces a shallow curve on the horizon like a hardly opened lid on the earth's cataract eye. It's hard to feel open in the cold.

Across three more crosswalks and through the back corridor between the civil engineering buildings, I walk with habitually tense knees and arches tuned to the plains and pimples of ice. The light is gone as my heels stretch up the long stairs of the college and the orbs of pedestrian street lamps reflect off the door handle. I knock my shoes together to dislodge the slush, unbutton my wool coat and unwrap the red chenille of my scarf. My neck feels open and vulnerable as the warmed cloth unwinds like a useless bandage.

Graduate Design Studio I is presenting today to close the semester and I've come to see the pinnacle. I dread the predictable trip to the Kitty Cat Klub that will inevitably follow and surely last too long. I can hear voices in the auditorium and swing the honeyed door open, pause in the high aisle, and shuffle past empty seats to one next to Häns. We whisper hellos. The graduate students are scattered down the incline like shale—relaxed after their individual critiques last week—the lights dimmed for slides. François turns around to whisper hi. "How was the Nutcracker?" I ask. "Good—I love Tchaikovsky, so much emotion. It's nice to have my dad back from China."

The group at the front finishes and François' group goes down to prepare their slides. Häns tells me who the critics are and settles into an open page of his sketchbook for notes. The lights dim again. I slide my coat off my shoulders and look around.

I start thinking of these people as architects and begin to notice things. Men. Leather shoes. Polished watches. Sweaters, colognes, stylish glasses. The masculine ease of a still mostly-masculine profession, their social effortlessness. No wonder it's notorious their clients' wives have affairs with them.

François' group begins and I notice he's listed on the title slide as 'Frank.' I shake my head—he's anything but a Frank. Born in France, raised in Paris, Belgium, China, and the States, at 25 he's played the violin for 13 years, lives in a loft downtown and dresses almost exclusively in Banana Republic. Everything he owns fits him. He introduces himself as Frank because he's gotten tired of being called Francis. I specifically call him only François; changing 'François' for 'Frank' represents to me sanction of American ethnocentrism. I refuse to do it.

Häns shifts in his chair and I notice for the first time what he's wearing today: green cargo pants with a bleached spot on the knee and a baggy yellow t-shirt. He's unshaven and his hair hasn't been cut for four months, the result equally of lack of time and lack of money. I know he's wearing cologne but I'm used to it and never smell it any more. He's listening intently to the group and sketching from their slides, taking notes in his uppercase letters.

The rest of the groups finish and people disappear to the studio for coats and bags. Everyone—critics and professors included—heads to the Kitty Cat to lounge and clink glasses. We walk the three blocks under lighted ginkgo trees separately, each hooked into different conversations. As the first married couple in our social clutch, we developed the habit of splitting at parties to combat the co-dependent, reflexive stereotype of newlyweds.

One of the few women students, an English major as an undergrad, and I strike up a conversation about the territoriality of writers. I glance at Häns, laughing with a classmate as his breath bursts out in a white cloud, and notice that out of the corner of my eye I'm keeping track of who François is talking to.

He's always talking. It annoys Häns, but I see it as one of the things they have in common: gregarious, expressive characters with a tendency to take conversation as batting practice rather than a series of volleys. I've learned with Häns this is more about excitement than self-centeredness. And I like these people—they save me from having to arrange and strategize a conversation. It's a relief from all the other performances I'm putting on this winter. And when the talker's not my husband I also get to stop analyzing and drop into my momentary self. The one who's not required to contextualize attitudes, replies, and statements into their long-term meanings and repercussions.

We all cross the street and flow into the club single file. Häns holds the door open for everyone and I thank him as I walk through—a formality that becomes a sort of intimacy because we both know my 'Thank you' stands out because it has a past and a future. We meet eyes and I smile a bit. Lately we're most at ease in public because it excuses us from facing or addressing our problems.

The Kitty Cat is the kind of lounge no one would visit if it was ever fully lit. The couches, upholstered in deeply textured, mismatched fabric, clump next to snake plants and spare ficus. The brick in the walls is exposed, and kitschy, light-up stars swoop around, dangling from the blades of ceiling fans. The place smells dusty and the bartenders and servers sport piercings and tattoos. The small stage, lit in red, hosts acoustic singer/songwriters and a few jazz trios. If you look at anything too long you begin to notice the place is not just antique, it's dirty. As precisely as they dress, architects tend to fancy themselves artists rather than technicians and the bohemian-by-association vibe seems to be what draws them here. That, and the two-for-one wine and imported beers for happy hour. It's one of those bars where the food is too expensive for the place to be truly alternative, but its masquerading as such makes everyone feel they're making artistic connections.

Häns offers to buy me a drink, a generous and constant sacrifice in our financial reality: a drink for me means none for him. I'm thirsty for water, a typical and diplomatic response in our conversational navigation: a drink for me means none for him.

"Really, go ahead babe—it's your last day of studio. I really am feeling dehydrated."

He sees there's heart in my reply, not just will, and heads to the bar to order. He's tired, I can see it in the way he walks—his arms bent, palm enfolding knuckles. At his most transparent moments he has a childlikeness about him, a wide-eyed, open-handed unassumption. It may be because his cheeks are a little round, but I think instead it's the way he considers things with absolute simplicity. To my husband, handing over money is no cause for regret and relationships do not involve tallies. He's the kind of man who makes me think 'sophisticated' shouldn't be an adjective I desire so much. Watching him take a bottle in each hand and promptly give one to a friend (whom he knows had a hard time making rent this month) I love him. It knocks a crack into my frozen cave. He's exactly the kind of man I want as a father to my children.

"Bonjour mademoiselle, comment allez-vous?" François saunters up and drapes his arm around my shoulders.

"Madame. *Madame.*" I say smiling. I've been acting for family and friends long enough cocktail pleasantness is no challenge. "Careful there." I tense my shoulders to keep the contact light. I know enough about François to know he doesn't always think of the implications of his words or actions. Häns shoots me a sympathetic smile—*that darn François*—and goes back to his conversation. Jealousy is one of the few issues we've never had. But I worry about appearing too open to the eyes of all the others: studios are

Petri dishes for gossip. To contextualize François' *faux pas* out of dangerous territory, I turn to wit.

"A Frenchman whose vocabulary is worse than an American girl's? François, I took three weeks of French in summer school in third grade—even I know that one."

He smiles and shows his rounded white teeth. His open demeanor makes propriety a requirement of mine not his. His amaretto clinks in his other hand and I notice he's wearing my favorite cologne. The smell is close and warm. I feel myself relax a little and, after being cold all day, suddenly notice his arm is warm resting over my nearly bare shoulders. I'm usually so far from my body Häns has to rub my shoulders for an hour before I remember I have skin. And here's my body—not even being asked to notice.

But I'm so tired of being watchful, of having problems to solve. Our physical problems make it necessary and pointless to be attentive to the meaning and implication of everything. For once, it's nice to have a feeling without a strategy.

I continue the conversation: "So, have you heard from the girl yet?"

François' dark eyebrows raise over his high cheekbones. He has a bright face, childlike in its own way, inquisitive and happy. This is a man for whom life has been relatively easy, for whom resources are never in question. Someone with confidence.

I prompt him: "The girl? From the party?" Still under his arm, I'm beginning to feel the warmth down my shoulders and across my chest. A clasp deep inside my ribs clicks open and my joints begin to feel more lithe. I breathe the amber light we're in and open to the room.

"No!" He frowns. "Letmetellyouwhathappened—" His arm lifts from my shoulder and pauses in a storytelling gesture. The rest of the architecture crowd has finished getting their drinks and circled in two groups. François and I stand apart by the stage next to a pool of red light. "So . . . Saturday I went out to a party and she was there—but," he shifts his shoulders to the other side, "her friend was there too. And . . . I kind of dated her friend for a while—"

"François!" I play the expected role. Out from under his arm, it feels colder in the room.

"I know . . . " François' chin lowers like a chastised puppy and he gives an apologetic smile. His hair is a European sort of brown, darker than brunette without being black. It's tactile, wavy and thick. I can feel it in the space between my fingers.

I realize I'm standing closer to him than I need to and glance around. Everyone else is engaged in their conversations, drinks in hands, ankles on knees. Häns is part of a quartet whose laughing punctuates the din. François and I sit on the edge of the stage to continue our conversation. The boards of the stage are orange in the red light and the rest of the bar, which I can see from this corner, seems dark in comparison. Separated and on a stage, I smell François' cologne again and begin to feel like here in front of everyone I'm getting away with something.

"Frank, are you a *good* guy?" I break all my roles and speak directly. This is a high stakes gamble. Whatever sea I'm beginning to feel lapping at my body, I know his answer could be a lifebuoy or an anchor. "Or are you just out to have a good time?"

His face gets serious and his brown eyes stare into his glass. This is a good sign—a bad sign.

"No, I'm a good guy." An unusual pause. "I actually end up getting walked on in a lot of relationships." I can see this. His energy is easily directed and he's eager to please. Materially he's had no reason in life to learn to be selfish, maybe this crosses over.

The conversation has also crossed over and I lost my gamble. I know because I feel like I've won. I throw out a question:

"So, what kind of girl are you really looking for then?" He'll toss out some features, some traits, and my lifelong insecurities will evaporate the rising amber. First he'll say tall, then blonde; he'll say something that will simultaneously discredit him in my eyes and me in his. *Me in his?*

He looks right into my eyes as he speaks, shoulders relaxed as he leans back onto his right arm. "She has to be ambitious—you know, want to *do* something with her life."

"Totally."

"My last girlfriend was too much TV."
"I hate TV."
"She wasn't interested in traveling—"
"You're kidding—it's only been a little over a year since I was in London to visit my sister and I feel like I'm going crazy."
"She wore a lot of sweatpants. Which is fine for hanging around and stuff, but we'd plan to go out for dinner and I'd show up dressed . . ." He gestures at his soft white button-down and crisp black pants.
"—Nice. Classy.—"
" . . . and she'd be in sweats."
"I don't even own a pair of sweatpants."
"And she wasn't interested in learning my language."
I shake my head. "That's hard if someone you care about isn't interested in working to learn your language." *Responsible, trustworthy*—in float words from a bilingual marriage. They suddenly marshal in phrases I don't believe in, seeds that have been thought but, miraculously, haven't germinated: *just outgrew it, incompatible*. "Or if they just can't."

François sips his drink and nods. When he sets it back down I get another wave of his warm smell. Another thought strikes him and as he begins to speak, his fingers touch my arm in a casual, unthought gesture. Looking at him my body is warm and comfortable, relaxed. I feel intelligent and confident. A starving part of me feels fed. He really does have beautiful eyes. I notice.

For the rest of the night I glance at Häns, keeping track of where he bounces in conversation, telling myself my looks are measures for his wellbeing not my self-protection. Feeling for the first time in months I have a self to protect.

All the next morning, while Häns and I shower together, I blabber about the party we're going to in the evening: how glad I am it's Friday, how I'm really in the mood to get out a little and have some fun for once.

Häns chuckles at this unusual morning burst while he dries his hair. "You're in a good mood."

"Well, aren't you excited to get out some? To celebrate being done? What do you think I should wear? Will people be dressed up or casual?" I swing my navy bathrobe around my shoulders. "I want to look good for you." I smile at him.

"Just wear that." He pulls on a pair of boxers.

"My bathrobe?" I tie the robe sash.

"What's underneath," he says, buttoning his jeans and popping his spiky head through a black t-shirt with a smirk.

"I'm guessing I'd be underdressed." I smirk back, rubbing my towel through my hair.

"You'd be the best dressed chicken there," he says, using my quirky nickname from a Kurt Vonnegut novel. He smiles and leaves the bathroom to make our coffee. I pick a fitted top with a draped neckline, black pants and sassy boots. Nice. Classy.

Back in the bathroom I pull my make-up bag from the top shelf of the medicine cabinet. The espresso machine in the kitchen—a luxury leftover from the days before Häns went back to school—squeals as he steams milk for lattés. I adjust my shirt, conscious of my breasts for the first time in days, and think, *I'm dressing for a man who's not my husband.* I'm so relieved to be excited about something I let the tingle ripple over my skin.

A glass of wine. Red. Ruby. Swirl. Sip. I can smell my own perfume. Red. Jasmine. Succulent. Sitting on the couch, legs crossed. Leaning over. "So, do you think of yourself as French or American?" Both really. "Favorite place you've lived?" Great house in Belgium. Took these vacations to the coast of Italy. THRUM: bass kicks the roots of my breath. Blows. Swells into the floor of my throat. Billie Holiday in remix, the music slinks like spirit, the treble skitters like static over spreading cirrus . . . *that lipstick . . . hush now, don't explain* . . . The middle reels, like a round lock racing, slipping. Sip. Warm oak. Black pepper. "Häns,—sorry to interrupt—you're going downstairs? Great. I'll come in a bit." Smooth wood floors, voices, scarves over the lamps. Candles burning somewhere. Close to his family. "And architecture?" More interested in development, really. A business man. Different cologne tonight. Sip. Say 'merlot.' The mouth moves like a kiss. People from the other end of the couch come and go, we stay. *I didn't tell him to sit here, did I?* Legs touching. Me: leaning over, wine glass in the left; talk, gesture; right hand (writing hand): fingertips touch his arm. Relaxed muscle under. THRUM: *lipstick . . . don't explain.*

More wine, madam? "Thank you, yes." I feel like I'm in a Rothko painting. A red one. Where it's warm. *What if this was my life?* A painting to make love in. Jessica joins our conversation. She's with Mike, *with* him. François jokes about stealing, luring. He's not serious. One arm around each of us. Sip. Is he? He leaves for a blonde. Left, we joke: always has to meet the new girl. We share our distain for the ones who giggle: Speak French, Speak French. Like it's some kind of cabaret.

Häns comes, smiling. He finally feels the semester is done. More wine for my baby? "Sure—the merlot. Be right back, I'm going to run to the bathroom." Kiss on the cheek. Step, step, step-step. My eyes in the mirror looking in my eyes. Blink, focus. You know what you're doing, don't you? You know what you're doing, don't you.

Dark. Empty green wine bottles in a cluster on the dining room table. Music. Heartbeat. François. THRUM: lock reels. Hips pulled in. Häns talking elsewhere. Top beat trips, treble orbits. Spin with the room. Hand in his hand. Hand on my back, palm, violin fingertips, press. Close. Palm on his arm, clutch, spin. His muscles beneath my fingers taut, loose. Spin. Hold. Hips locked. Breathe. Sweat. Drop. Chest open. Neck arched. Fall. Catch, his hot hand open, arm cradle. Sweeping. Up. The heat from his chest on my breast. THRUM. The smell of his skin, tan. The space between hot, humming. Red. Inside, the deep strokes of red on grey. Slow. To. Sway. Fingers guide, wrapped into. My side, encircled. Held. My fingers stretch in his hand, feel it. He smiles, brown eyes open.

Floor turns. Axis between. Force pushes, he pulls. Faster. Force pushes, he pulls, tension locks. Firm. Rushing. Resistance makes the solid thing. Spin flies open, fall back, sweating. Laughing.

2 am. Drunk, warm, happy. *If I was here alone. Whose home?* Party mellows. Häns happy to see me happy: We better go, babe, . . . morning . . . class. Smiling at him, limbs loose: "But I don't want to go." Häns happy I'm happy, with his friends. François scoops me up, easy fit, carries me to Häns. Smile: Votre épouse, monsieur. Häns, smile: Merci. *Trois.* They are taking care of me. Spinning touch: carry home. I'm the conjunction. "But, I don't want to go." I don't want to go. Home.

For a month after the party, Häns and I have spectacular sex. Neither of us ask any questions. I wonder about the risks God is willing to take, about the haunting of a tattered old prayer.

"Betsy, this is April. We need to talk." I paced between the bed and the window, behind the closed door of the bedroom, talking to her voicemail. "Something you said yesterday caught me and if it means what I think it might, we need to have a conversation."

The next afternoon, she came over after work and sat on my living room couch. The last time we'd talked about our marriages, she had let out a string of words that started my brain sliding: "at that point we were pretty much already committed." There was only one action I could imagine she'd interpret as an obligation to marriage. Sex.

We didn't hug when she showed up, and automatically sat on opposite sides of the room. I laid out the pieces, told her the picture I was starting to see. She didn't deny it, but she didn't say the words either.

I was so mad my hands shook.

For God's sake, I'd given her a sex talk. Had sat in front of her days before her wedding and said "be sure you're really relaxed," "you'll probably need to use some KY or something." Tried to say things that would give them a better chance, save them from the year of—the year we'd had. Had sacrificed my experience to say, "Whatever happens, try to remember things can be okay." And she'd sat there and listened. Thanked me for it.

On the couch, she looked me in the eye and said she never lied about it. I gagged on my own spit.

"So if Brian—if Brian ran out and kissed another woman he wouldn't be lying to you if he just didn't *mention* it? I was supposed to sit you down and *ask*? I stood with you at your wedding and had no *idea* what you were dealing with."

"My wedding was fine. I was forgiven and pure."

And your best friends had no idea you'd ever been otherwise.

"It was between us and God."

And I've shared the hell of my sex life with you because I *had* to? Because it was somehow your *right* to hear it?

She looked me in the eye the whole time, smug, defensive. It made me furious. Like the experience had given her some kind of queenly knowledge. Like they'd earned their great sex life for suffering through something I wouldn't understand. Like breaking the rules gave them rights, made her wise. The facts of her life mocked the holes in mine.

And she'd been modest. Played the pastor's wife. Wore long skirts and reprimanded Heidi for swearing too much. Was 'concerned' my husband showed up with a six pack whenever we came over. Brian was a pastor—a pastor. Sat in front of teenagers and told them they needed to be real about God and the things in their lives.

And I'd bought it—had reexamined my wardrobe and tracked how often Häns cracked open a Summit when he came home. Had admired Brian's bravery in opening his life to teenagers with such transparency. Had considered that the entire reason I couldn't make love with my husband was that I was too selfish to really give.

I didn't watch her leave, didn't wave when she pulled out of the driveway. Paced in the bathroom, feverish, heart burned, ready to vomit.

Fuck you. You and this sham of a religion. You and the gaggle of men who prance around youth groups telling the girls to dress right so the boys don't lust. Who don't even say lust. Who say 'stumble'—as if they were tripped.

You and your weak army of men, pussyfooting around pornography without the balls to stand up and shut it down. With your chins dragging over the floor, mouths open, after a flat glossy picture. Shove it down your throat.

And get on your great high horse, your knight's horse, to damn those girls and their abortions, to banner their selfishness and immaturity. Do it. Do it. Fly those banners high. And raise your eyebrows when someone says 'rape.' But don't stain those white-gloved hands to raise a banner about that. That shouldn't be discussed.

Fuck you. Fuck you for being some kind of man—for calling childbirth a woman's redemption, for cornering women in nurseries and children's classrooms, for filling apocalypse with a gendered evil.

And all the other books your men publish, about praying wives, woman's hearts, mother's souls. Call it 'Women's Ministry' to differentiate it from the real kind.

Then spend a good long retreat bemoaning your wives' lack of adventure in the bedroom. Sit perplexed those long skirts and one sacred nod toward the motherly and industrious don't ignite a holy passion. Leave them bone dry.

And encourage those women to get good and mad at each other. To twitter and gossip over the one you all look at. To blame her.

And you, go ahead and sit in your heaven and pass your rewards as you please. I know whose side you're on now, you tyrannous father, you loveless bridegroom, you impotent ghost. And it's not mine.

"Who wants a shake? Mocha, strawberry, vanilla—make your claim."

Wednesday night, another finals week and Häns has plenty of company in the studio. The place is trashed: plots and pizza boxes, chunks of Styrofoam, dowels, tin ventilation tubes, cardboard, Plexiglas, basswood. Ribbons of trace paper lace the tables

Holy Ghosts

and spiny pins tack site photographs, digital renderings, and Prismacolor sketches up over desks and drawing tables. Drafting lines and curves jut out drawers, and network cables and power cords snake across the floor to laptops and elbowed mechanical lamps. The laptops take turns blasting 80s ballads, movie theme songs, club house, salsa and the Beatles.

By this point in Häns' program, I feel like the studio mother. I bring food, keep up on everyone's progress and sympathize over sickness and harsh critiques. I know the security code for the studio door and have spent at least one whole night on one of the third-hand mismatched couches. I grade papers here when I can, bring reading, and help brainstorm conceptual words for titles and presentation boards. Häns and I have learned to classify this as spending time together because there's just no other way to survive it.

My visit tonight is a surprise—an 11 pm drop-in after my night class, a study break in the round-the-clock timesheet of studio. I hand out the shakes and pull a chair up next to Häns at one of the work tables. He's modeling intricate prismatic ceiling trusses in two-foot sections. He and the rest of the studio ridicule the gigantic scale for this project: 1/4" = 1'. It makes all their projects seem like Tinker Toys. I've brought a stack of textbooks to review in preparation for the next semester of composition.

Todd, the California surfer boy who's really from Fargo, has gone a little loopy already in the night, and kicks off a round of mocking and therapeutic impersonations of instructors. The rest of the crew, from spots at tables, desks, laptops, and squares of floor pitch in lines and gestures for a menagerie. The session goes downhill fast to the hypothesis studio is a microcosm of the world: the professors, various breeds of intellectuals; Todd, of course, is the surfer-type; Sonja, the hippie; Jen, the representation of all things Asian (which she doesn't appear to mind); François,

"Well, the French are dicks." Ryan, Häns' partner in representing the working class, punchlines. The joke hits: François is hardly around, works from home, and has drawn contempt from the peanut butter sandwiches and PBR majority for never having to worry about making rent. I hate the spite in this and think about retaliating: So, Häns and Ryan, what are you two? The Bible Belt?

The session passes and everyone falls back into working. I take the moment to tell Häns about my good news for the day: I may be offered a course in creative writing for the next semester.

"The email said that—"

"Done!" He stands up and holds one truss up to the other. "Todd—look, two down."

I pause waiting for him to reenter my story. He doesn't.

A few minutes later I try again. "So, I think I may have found a—"

Häns pops his head up. "That's Sonja's—she's building another one." He's responding to another conversation. I decide to leave. There's no sense in sticking around just to get more irked with him. He's had a long week. I've had a long week. I've learned this time of year makes me needy and gives him a short attention span. It's a bad combination and I know, from experience, trying to talk about it now will only exacerbate the situation. But, now that I've identified I feel ignored, I won't be able to disregard it if it keeps happening. Naming is dangerous for me. Once I name something, I infuse it with intention; if I can identify what he's doing, he must be doing it on purpose. In my better moments I see this is ridiculous and I separate before my emotions can make the equation. This is one of my better moments.

Häns is oblivious, which is probably better, and he walks me to the car to say goodnight. The air feels clean for the city, as it often does here at night, and the frat houses are unusually quiet. We kiss and he says he'll cuddle in when he gets home around two. I'm sure it will be later, but there's no sense in dashing his optimism when he's got so many hours to go.

"Love you, babe. Drive careful."

"Love you too—I'm proud of you. Good luck." He walks down the sidewalk back toward school and I scoop our Golf in a u-turn toward 4th Street. At the stop sign I remember an earlier thought. Waiting in line for the shakes, I'd toyed with the idea of bringing one to François at his place. I recognize the thought for what it is: a mind trained toward possibilities making a juvenile and desperate attempt to see a crush. I turn onto 4th and flick on the radio to pack away the thought.

As if on some cue, familiar notes drift from the speakers. What are the chances. For days after that winter party I listened for a certain R&B song that carried an emotional echo. Now, five months later, here it is.

I slow the Golf for a red light. The streetlights on 4th stretch down the hills like a runway, to François' place. Where he is. Alone.

It's midnight. All I have to do is drive straight. Straight down 4th, into the city. The red lava lamp in his fourth floor window above the iron railroad bridge. The timber pillars inside. The open loft with its high ceilings and concrete floors. The lamp on at his desk, where he sits piecing together a model.

I pass the blur of another light. All I have to do is keep driving straight, bring him something—say I brought food to studio but he wasn't there so I wanted to be sure he didn't miss out. Say I dropped by on my way home to check in.

Two lights pass in the haze of my thoughts: None of it would be unusual, we've been to the loft a dozen times. Driving, parking, buzzing in, none of it would even be unnatural. Then, to ride up the elevator, walk down the angled hall and knock on door 406.

I look good tonight, laid back. Jeans with vines embroidered at the pockets, boots that make my slender hips sway, light v-neck sweater. Black bra. Something warm and liquid drops straight through me. I shift into fourth.

If I went this one time, what would keep it from happening again? No one expects François to be at studio. Clearly. No one expects me to be anywhere. And if this one anomaly, me showing up alone, passed, what others would go in progression? What if he wasn't surprised when I knocked on the door? What if he had thought about it?

Or, if it didn't matter what he had thought about. There's power in my body. Underneath the scab of religion, those crusted rules of chastity, there's a lithe, supple flesh. And it's mine. Mine.

Not some husband's to do with what he pleases. Not some God's to string and drain.

The streetlights smear by.

Weeks ago it would have been 'Betsy would kill me' and I would have cared. Killing something in myself while she sat happy in her self-fulfilled belief nothing ever has to die.

The light is red. I downshift, third, second, first. The street unblurs, the edges of the street sign against the black sky cut my brain from its high buzzing wires and snap it to place.

To place: here in the turn lane. Signal clicking right, out of simple habit.

I want to scream. I can't even cry. My body does this to save my marriage? Years of effort to feel a kiss and the neurons fire for this? To get to a blinking signal. To take me to an empty home. *Damn you and your haunting. You won't show up. You won't leave me alone.*

Two and a half weeks later, on a May evening, Häns and I sit at a metal mesh table on the patio of a downtown pub to begin an evening out for his 26th birthday. The air is soft and bluish and it's early enough in the spring the sound of traffic is still refreshing. Simply being able to sit outside makes it feel like a holiday.

The traffic lights run their rounds and the other patio tables fill as the skyscrapers shift their shadows over the sidewalks. I can see the street from where I sit, the people walking by. There's a strange stint in the road at the next intersection, one that's not quite perpendicular—the kind where you don't know which direction you're actually going until you get to the crossroads because the directions aren't in opposites.

Next to me, Häns slides his chair in and out, shuffling up to greet people as they come and screeching chairs and tables across the concrete to make more seats. François sits on my right, ordering a drink, and across from me Betsy and Brian confer about ordering dinner. I can't figure out how we all ended up at the same table.

In a wacky sort of twist, François has become Brian's band's biggest fan. Häns and I introduced them a few months ago, and now they're talking about having a concert in the basement party room of the loft. After our blowout, neither Betsy or I knew what to do, so in a strange inertia we've kept running into each other. I got angry and things kept going. With his birthday floating, Häns and I haven't fought, and even though I took that turn toward home, I keep smelling sandalwood and following it into conversation with François.

My sister and her husband show up and when I come back from greeting them, Brian, Betsy, François, and I begin to talk about God. Amidst the bar chatter, François ends up saying he doesn't believe in God. Betsy asks why, and he says something about the harm religion has done to so many people. I nod. He seems more embarrassed about saying what he doesn't believe in than what he does and looks up from his drink to tell about his experience two years ago with a wakeboarding neck injury.

"It gave me a new perspective—that you just have to live fully. You can't waste time wondering about things. You have to do what you want and really enjoy the things in your life."

Brian nods. The story is fresh to him and Betsy. I've heard about the accident, the recovery before, but never the spiritual side of it.

"Did you ever feel taken care of?" I ask. "Watched out for? Lying in the hospital bed, waking up and knowing you were okay?"

"I could feel the love of my family, so strong—I knew they were taking care of me."

I wonder about displacement. How we credit the things we feel. Where we place them, what we call them.

I sense Betsy is going to ask François how he knows it wasn't God. I feel like her saying it that way would ruin something, reduce some truth he's telling about his experience. Would mean if you don't call an experience something it's not that thing. Or that each experience can only have one name: love or duty, spirit or body, God or human. Betsy feels love and calls it God, calls it God in the face of everything. Even now, after months of carelessly unprotected sex, she sees her swelling breasts and belly as direct results of God's provision—finds it the wellspring of comfort and counsel.

And on the other side of the table, François' healed body and protected spirit have nothing to do with God. He praises the smarts of doctors, the network that made a path to a skillful surgeon. Feels the strong force that watched over as a power among, between, people—finds comfort and help spoken in the language of the communion of human hands.

The server arrives with platters of fish and chips, and the conversation is over. But I want to go back in, want to stop the logic of all the silverware shuffling, birthday wishing, traffic whirring, and say, But which one do you have to believe in more—the experience or its name? And what about you: the sex, the choice to ride on water? What about your power? How can I possibly, on this map of choice and detour, determine who is steering?

Monday I drive down 4th, ride up the elevator, walk down the angled hall, and knock on door 406.

The daylight in the loft is beautiful: soft cream sheen on the polished concrete, ivory gloss on the walls, the smoke of incense floating in the open space like tender branches. The skyline out the window is silver and reflective. The sound of the traffic outside, below the open windows, is muffled and prosaic. Inside everything feels washed.

François and I stand in the center in the middle of the day, talking. I'm dressed for work—my black sandals by the door, red coat on over my black skirt and silk sweater. He's in jeans and a button-down, talks with his hands in his back pockets. I keep my hands mostly in mine. The loft is bright and everything feels open and clean.

I've brought a gift—a thank you for having people at his place later in the evening on Häns' birthday and for an over-generous bottle of French cognac. The bed is neatly made. A water glass rests in the sink. We talk.

Holy Ghosts

He seems humbled by the gift. I say 'we' appreciate it and it just means so much to 'us' he was willing to have people over at the last minute. Conversation is easy and unforced. Like we could sit down in the nook of the couch in the light and talk all afternoon.

We hug as I turn to leave, then stand by the counter and talk for ten more minutes. The open gift box and tissue lay spread across the polished granite, the new vase set already in its place on a simple shelf above the bed.

When I finally need to leave for class, François opens the door and I walk into the white hall and say a final thanks. I turn and walk toward the elevator.

There's no sound in the hall. Then, finally, from the elevator lobby, I hear his blonde door click and I try not to look behind it, for pause, for sigh, for relief. I turn around in the elevator and watch the blank face couple.

I have no final name to say—God, me, love, duty, spirit, flesh—and it gives me no one to blame. This intermingling coexistence steals my native satisfaction, all my natural supply of worth. What it offers in return doesn't feel like comfort, power, or help. Neither like passion or obligation. Merely breath: one pull to the gut, one push into the world.

Separation is what has come undone.

Outside, the car starts too loud, the radio intrusive. The sun begins to drop below the stormy clouds of the day, full, burnt, quiet. I pull into the city street and try not to notice the underside of the sunset is burning, orange and smoldering, dark, and deeper than the light.

I pick up my phone to dial Häns' number, cross the iron bridge, and try to account for this dark loneliness in being never alone.

Häns and I stand at the front of the church next to Betsy and Brian, little Ella wrapped up in Betsy's arms, stretching her foot out when she stirs. Three weeks ago I saw that foot the moment she was born—toes spread wild with the cold and motion—Betsy next to me hot and finally still, the smell of blood musky in the room. My body dripped its month and while I stroked her hair ("You can do it, Betsy, your little girl is coming, your daughter's coming,") Betsy's tore a tide.

They have asked us to be Ella's godparents, models of the ways of faith to help them raise their daughter. Betsy fears the ways parents can sentence their children and wants her daughter to have another image of a woman trying to live in faith. Me.

In the service, the pastor talks about community and I know the question is coming. All around us faces wait, for the questions, the baptism, the food of fellowship to come after. Already I want to take Ella from the crowd. I want to grab her, take her away and whisper to her all the things she should know: that people lie, that she is loved. The things she should know absolutely.

Häns stands next to me, both of us too solemnly dressed from unfamiliarity with infant baptisms, and we hold hands. The arrangement of the font puts us at the center of the stage—another couple holding hands at the top of a church aisle. I'm afraid of the question that's coming, not because of the child coming with it, but because it's like being asked to choose my life over again. We. Will. With.

I watch Ella sleep in Betsy's arms and think about all the sorting she hasn't done yet. She sleeps in the day and wakes at night; weeps for any kind of hunger, whether people or food; recognizes only provision as love, doesn't consider it could be anything other. And, here, we mark her untouchable soul with—hands, people, water—all that's closest to touch.

The pastor says something about the light of the baptism candle, the church's hope each child will grow in love and knowledge.

I think of the nights after Ella's birth of not sleeping. The nights I sat up on the couch trying to make sense in those hours, as my husband stirred in my bed and my best friend nursed her child, of all the ways the body had just proven it could join every thing it tore apart. I didn't have a child, may never have a child, but I sat in my dark living room knowing, after that birth, that blood can join in ways that hands can never. And feeling like I'd witnessed a car wreck, I looked at my life and thought of all the cutting it took to get to blood.

The pastor turns from talking to the congregation, checks his notes, and looks at Häns and me. In the moment he checks his notes, I remember the event—that this includes grandmothers and crockpots and needing to clean up. And I know, with that question coming, the only thing I can say is yes. As much as I want to take this little girl and steal her away from everything—for her sake, for mine—I will let her go to the grandmothers that deserve to be proud and the guests that deserve to give wishes and I will find my way to the kitchen to do what needs to be done.

"And now, Godparents: Do you promise to demonstrate an authentic Christian faith to this child? To help bring Ella to worship and understanding? To teach her God's Word, and by your example, to show her the way to a personal relationship of faith?"

Häns squeezes my hand and we answer as the liturgy demands, "We will, and we ask God to help and guide us." And I know 'we,' 'will,' and 'with' mean an acquiescence, a certain kind of failure, just the way remembering crockpots means forgetting how much I want to sing this child all she should know. But I also know this way, as much as it can be misunderstood, is a way to make my love make space for more love.

The pastor turns to Brian and Betsy and takes Ella from Betsy's arms. He palms water from the silver bowl of the font and drips it onto Ella's tiny head, her eyes closed and her neck resting in his palm.

"Ella Joy, I baptize you in the name of the Father, the Son, and the Holy Spirit."

Amen.

ACKNOWLEDGMENTS

Memoir is often understood as one person's story. Instead, crafting a book from a lived life acknowledges most how our lives are braided—how the thread of my story begins before me, interweaves with others' along the way, and will continue on the loom after my colors have faded. These are my words, but this story is the work of many, to whom I offer gratitude for the texture and richness of this book and this life:

Thanks to *Ruminate* and Brianna Van Dyke for first believing these words had a place in the world and initially publishing excerpts as "40 Days" in Issue 13: Confession, 2009 and "Taizé" in Issue 17: Pilgrimage, 2010.

To my family, who have borne much of the cost of creating this story: Thank you, Häns, for your years of support and encouragement. Sören and Gwyn, thank you for your inspiration and grace in sharing my energy with work you don't yet understand.

Thank you to the people who allowed their lives to be shared here. Mom and Dad, Megan and Mindy, Brian and Betsy. Your willingness to gift your lives—to allow your stories to be shaped by another, in so many ways— is one of the most enduring testaments in my life to the power of vulnerability and trust and the mysterious ways of redemption. You are the cloud of witnesses.

Vicki Cary, your teaching was the foundation. Thank you for the enduring gift of competence.

Acknowledgments

Deborah Keenan, thank you for existing. You are a force for good in the literary universe; so many of us would not have found gravity without you. I'll never live up to your generosity.

Joey Horstman, many thanks for not laughing at my undergraduate work, for teaching good literary taste, and for critical lessons in self-respect.

Marion Larson, thank you for forthright feedback, and taking me seriously enough to bring notes.

Daniel Taylor, my thanks for helping me stumble though the business of writing with some portion of your aplomb.

Michael Holmes, thank you for lending your considerable expertise to checking my use of Koine Greek.

De Zhang, thank you for information and insight on Mandarin Chinese given in authentic collegiality.

Kelsey Widman, my publication assistant, thank you for your energetic engagement, insight, creative thinking, and diligence. It's been a joy to work with you. Your smarts and enthusiasm have made this work better.

Matthew Wimer, Christian Admonson, and the staff at Wipf & Stock, thank you for opening a gate to allow this work into the wider world.

To the Arts Collective of Woodland Hills Church in St. Paul, thank you for sustaining creative community—for mucking around in the daily, gritty, inglorious work of striving to expand the territory where Beauty reigns. Thank you, especially, Craig Evans, Joanna Hallstrom, DeAnne Parks, Ruth Richmond, Anthony Vogel, Gregg Ward, Alyssa Whiting and Greg Wollan: I'm inspired, challenged and borne up by the faithful making in your lives.

Jessica Henderson, thank you for creative and expert mentorship of the design students at Bethel University who created and developed cover designs: Heidi Kao, Brita MacInnes, Allegra Rose, and Emily Swanberg. And thanks to Lex Thompson for sharing your photography expertise.

Heidi Kao and Emily Swanberg, the cover designers for *Triptych*, thank you for your deep consideration of my story, inspiring

Acknowledgments

conversation, excellent craftsmanship, enduring professionalism, and selfless commitment to this project.

Readers, past and present: Thank you for listening. I'm honored you have taken my words into your life. May you find grace and beauty, adventure and homecoming, in your own matches of faith.

DISCUSSION QUESTIONS

1. In the prologue, the author questions the common metaphor of faith as a journey and calls faith, instead, "a match: a puzzle, a flame, a fight." How do the metaphors we use to frame our spiritual lives affect our spiritual experiences? How might these metaphors help us? How might they limit us?

2. How does the language used in the faith of our childhoods affect our lifelong experience of God? How might favored names for God, for example, or the formality of religious language affect faith formation?

3. The author encounters different aspects of God predominantly at different ages in her life. Do you think this is common in the experience of faith through the lifespan? How does our conception of God change as we age? How might our own developmental stage affect how much (and what) we are able to understand? What threads connect your younger and older ways of thinking about God?

4. We often think of the human as being made of body, mind and spirit. What does this story say about unity, division and proportion of those aspects? Does it change in the author's life as she grows? In what way? Is this a change you've experienced?

Discussion Questions

5. How did place (the farm, China, Taizé, Paris, etc.) shape the author's spiritual experience? How has it shaped yours? In what ways does landscape cultivate our spiritual lives?

6. What happens to the author's fears—both spiritual and relational—as she grows? Do they shift, evolve, deepen, dissipate, etc.? Why do you think that happened?

7. What does this story say about the territories of love and duty? Is doing what "should be done" a help or a hindrance to authentic spiritual experience? How does that compare to loyalty to duty in authentic relationships between people?

8. There are many kinds of prayer in this story: informal, liturgical, public, private, silent, spoken, still, active. What can the form of prayer contribute to the experience of prayer?

9. How did the messages the author received about femininity affect the formation of her identity? How did they affect the formation of her faith?

10. This story of a woman's faith formation and struggle is mostly populated by men. How does that seem appropriate or inappropriate to you?

11. Our relationships with the people in our lives, who are embodied, affect our relationships with God, who is not embodied to us now. How does the incarnation frame, ease, or complicate the interplay of these relationships?

12. What do you think about the ways the narrator expressed her anger toward God? What about the ways she expressed her love?

13. *Triptych* illustrates some of the ways human relationships can impact our relationship with God. What does that influence make you consider or question about our relationships to each other?

14. What changed between the scene where the author considers visiting Francois and the scene where she does visit him?

Discussion Questions

15. How much emotional connection to God is required for a person's faith to be "real"? What experiences in your life lead you to that conclusion?

16. The "unreliable narrator" is an established literary device. In what ways do you think the author might see herself as an unreliable narrator?

17. The author accuses God of not being on her side. What do you think of this desire of hers to have God on her side, rather than vice versa?

18. At her goddaughter's baptism the author affirmed commitments that were in conflict with her emotions. What does that say about this woman? About her God? About the use or complication of formal affirmations of faith?

19. "Amen" is often defined as meaning "so be it; truly." It also expresses both an ending and a wish. What does the "Amen" at the end mean? At the close of this story, what is being affirmed? What is being ended? What is being hoped?

NOTES

Fathers

Lyrics from "I'll Be a Sunbeam." Words by Nellie Talbot. Public Domain.

The story of Daniel and the Lion's Den from Daniel 6:1–28.

The biblical text for the Christmas story comes from Luke 2:1–9, 15–20. Abbreviations have been made of verses 15–20.

Sons

Quoted text in the prayer is Matthew 7:7, 8.

The final verses of Malachi are Malachi 4:6.

The Chinese character 觅 (mì) means both "to search" and "to find" and contains the character for "seeing."

The story of Chang'e's ascent to the moon belongs to traditional Chinese mythology. Several versions of the tale are told. Chang'e is also known as Chang-o and Heng'e.

Song lyrics from "O Come, O Come, Immanuel." Author unknown, translation by John M. Neale.

The scripture on stones and bread comes from Matthew 7:9–11.

Ryan's reading on the kingdom of God comes from Luke 17:20–21. The opening lines of the parables, in order of mention, are found at: Matthew 13:24, 31, 44, 47, 18:23, 20:1, 22:2, 25:1, 14.

Notes

The Spanish quotation of John 21:25 is a paraphrase translated by Kit Johnson.

Holy Ghosts

Betsy quotes from 1 Corinthians 7:4.

www.ingramcontent.com/pod-product-compliance
Lightning Source LLC
Chambersburg PA
CBHW072149160426
43197CB00012B/2316